What Is God?

What Is God?

JACOB NEEDLEMAN

JEREMY P. TARCHER/PENGUIN

a member of Penguin Group (USA) Inc.

New York

JEREMY P. TARCHER/PENGUIN
Published by the Penguin Group
Penguin Group (USA) Inc., 375 Hudson Street, New York, New York 10014, USA ·
Penguin Group (Canada), 90 Eglinton Avenue East, Suite 700, Toronto, Ontario M4P 2Y3,
Canada (a division of Pearson Penguin Canada Inc.) · Penguin Books Ltd, 80 Strand,
London WC2R 0RL, England · Penguin Ireland, 25 St Stephen's Green,
Dublin 2, Ireland (a division of Penguin Books Ltd) · Penguin Group (Australia),
250 Camberwell Road, Camberwell, Victoria 3124, Australia
(a division of Pearson Australia Group Pty Ltd) · Penguin Books India Pvt Ltd,
11 Community Centre, Panchsheel Park, New Delhi–110 017, India ·
Penguin Group (NZ), 67 Apollo Drive, Rosedale, North Shore 0632, New Zealand
(a division of Pearson New Zealand Ltd) · Penguin Books (South Africa) (Pty) Ltd,
24 Sturdee Avenue, Rosebank, Johannesburg 2196, South Africa

Penguin Books Ltd, Registered Offices: 80 Strand, London WC2R 0RL, England

First trade paperback edition 2011
Copyright © 2009 by Jacob Needleman

Selections from *Tales of the Hasidim: The Early Masters* by Martin Buber, translated by Olga Marx, copyrighted
1947, 1948, and renewed 1975 by Schocken Books. Used by permission of Schocken Books, a division of
Random House, Inc.

Selections from *The Gnostic Religion* by Hans Jonas, copyright © 1958 by Hans Jonas. Reprinted by permission
of Beacon Press, Boston.

Selection from "Freedom: The Reality of Religion," pp. 268–269 in *Epistle to the Romans*, by Karl Barth, sixth
edition, edited by Edwyn Hoskins (translator), © 1972. Used by permission of Oxford University Press, Inc.

Most Tarcher/Penguin books are available at special quantity discounts for bulk purchase for sales
promotions, premiums, fund-raising, and educational needs. Special books or book excerpts also can be
created to fit specific needs. For details, write Penguin Group (USA) Inc. Special Markets,
375 Hudson Street, New York, NY 10014.

The Library of Congress catalogued the hardcover edition as follows:

Needleman, Jacob.
What is God? / Jacob Needleman.
p.   cm.
Includes bibliographical references and index.
ISBN 978-1-58542-740-6
1. God.   I. Title.
BL473.N44   2009   2009036614
211—dc22

ISBN 978-1-58542-847-2 (paperback edition)

Printed in the United States of America
1   3   5   7   9   10   8   6   4   2

Book design by Claire Naylon Vaccaro

FOR BENJAMIN AND IDA NEEDLEMAN

Acknowledgments

For this book, more than for any other I have written, I have received help from a great many friends and colleagues at every stage of its writing from its initial conception to its completion. They know who they are and here I want only to make sure they know how deeply grateful I am for their willingness to read what were sometimes only fragmentary pieces and undeveloped lines of thought and narrative. The very fact that throughout the writing of this book so many friends were "listening in" was a tremendous support, quite apart from their comments and criticism. I can't explain exactly why it was like this, but it was so. I had always believed that writing was fundamentally a solitary craft and no doubt it often is. But in my case, with this book, the steady atmosphere of attention and good will from so many others was from the outset a companionate presence.

That said, I wish to make special mention of the help I received from Roger Lipsey, who went through every page, paragraph and sentence of the first draft with a flaming sword in one hand and a sweet-sounding bell in the other. Both the sword and the bell made my heart glad (and my thought clearer) in equal measure.

I am more and more grateful that Mitch Horowitz remains my editor at Tarcher/Penguin. How has he managed so richly to support my efforts? I am not speaking only of his indispensable affirmation of what I am trying. What I now so clearly see and so deeply appreciate is also his ability to respect the reader with whom I am hoping to communicate and thereby to remind me of my ideals and obligations as a writer living in two worlds.

My wife, Gail: always there, always at my side, always understanding my aim even when I have nearly forgotten it, always wise and unafraid to speak from her conscience to mine. Such love.

Contents

Part Three

Part Four

Part One

CHAPTER ONE

My Father's God

To think about God is to the human soul what breathing is to the human body.

I say to think about God, not necessarily to believe in God—that may or may not come later.

I say: to think about God.

I clearly remember the moment something deep inside me started breathing for the first time. Something behind my thoughts and my desires and fears, something behind my self, something behind "Jerry," which was and is my name, the name of *me,* from my earliest childhood.

I can say this now, more than sixty years after my first conscious experience of this second breathing, this first breathing of the soul.

Let me explain.

The year is 1943. I am eight years old.

It is dark night, full summer in Philadelphia, hot, humid. I am aware that my father is sitting outside on the front steps.

We have only just moved into these small rooms on this bare, newly constructed street pretentiously named Park Lane.

The street is an island of low-rent apartments in a sea of wealth: leafy streets, large, gracious old houses—and all embraced by Philadelphia's incomparable Fairmount Park with its stretches of untamed forest and its rushing, mystical Wissahickon Creek.

I go down the thinly carpeted stairs and gingerly open the screen door, trying not to disturb my father's silence. I had thought to walk up the street into the sweet air of the park entrance. But this time, I don't know why, without a word, I sit down next to my father. I had never done that before. His solitudes were never inviting, often following bursts of anger or simply mysterious and, to me, a child, inexplicable. Always more or less frightening.

I sit down, noticing that his head is tilted toward the sky.

In front of us stretches a vacant lot, part of which my father has cultivated as a "victory garden" (during World War II the government asked citizens to help the war effort in that way to reduce pressure on the nation's food supply). In that garden, now enveloped in darkness, there live corn, carrots, cucumbers, tomatoes, radishes, lettuce, scallions, string beans and much else, planted and unplanted, some of it contained by the wooden fence and some of it rampantly flourishing in the wild lot behind the fence: lowly weeds with frost-green, sticky leaves, white-tufted milkweed, crowds of dandelions, and—to me most important of all—buzzing, brilliant insects, butterflies, some like fluttering snowflakes, others like flying wildflowers and others colored like jungle creatures, all heartbreakingly gentle and beautiful; snails, spiders, big, angry horseflies—and, lord of everything, the pale green praying mantis suddenly appearing out of nowhere in a moment of grace, as from another universe, so near on the leaf, so still, so complex, so seemingly conscious and wondrously deadly. And then, closest to my heart, grasshoppers—dancing, leaping, flying, singing grasshoppers, some earnest, some clownish, some as thick as my thumb, others almost as tiny as a crumb of bread in the palm of my hand. It brought tears of wonder and love to my eyes to see the identical intricate structure of this improbable creature written in both the tiniest dot of being and the largest individual member of the species.

Out there, now, occupying the whole of the soft darkness: fireflies—we called them "lightning bugs." Hundreds of them, intensifying the darkness by randomly glowing and vanishing in the same present moment; intensifying the silence with their noiseless rhythms of illumination. Like flickering stars they were, here, on earth.

But it was when I looked up into the sky that, at that moment, *I* appeared. It did not happen right away. Out of the corner of my eye I saw that my father was still looking up. And so I kept my gaze upward, noticing the stars, some of which formed into constellations whose names I knew. Imitating my father, I kept my gaze upward, just looking.

And suddenly, incomprehensibly, all at once, despite the heavy summer air that always absorbs most of the starlight—suddenly, as if by magic, the black sky was instantly strewn with millions of stars. Millions of points of light. Millions of worlds. Never, before or since, have I seen such a night sky, not even in remote mountains on clear nights. It was not simply that my eyes had become normally adjusted to the darkness; it was as though an entirely new instrument of seeing had all at once been switched on within me. Or, as it also seemed, as though the whole universe itself suddenly opened its arms to me, saying to me: "Yes, I am here. See, this is what I really am! Do you like my beautiful garment?"

In an instant, less than an instant, a powerful, neutral current of electricity streaked down both sides of my spine—so quickly I had not a moment to have a thought about it or an emotional reaction to it. Many years had to pass before I was able to understand something about what it was that came down through me.

My eyes stayed riveted on the millions of stars, the millions of tiny stars with hardly a black space between them.

I wondered about my father, but I didn't dare turn my head to look at him, afraid that these millions of worlds might somehow not be there when I turned back to them.

I don't know how long we both continued to sit there, silently. But finally, speaking in a voice that I had never heard from him before, he said:

"That's God."

Something, *someone* suddenly appeared in me, as new and different as the voice of my father was new and different. As though I were summoned into being by that new voice from outside and inside myself. I remember it as clearly now as though it has just happened: I saw my thoughts slowing down and some-how becoming longer and thinner, like an attenuating gray cloud, gradually dissolving, leaving a nearly blank, dark space in my mind. And then, one thought, one question, appeared and filled my mind: What is God? What am I? It was the same question, it was one question, one experience.

And yet, at the same time, it was also one answer, the same answer. And only years and years later did I begin to understand that experience and that answer: *I am.*

But there, sitting on the steps next to my father, I did not have those words. I kept my head up and my eyes upturned, but already the millions of stars were fading away as mysteriously as they had appeared. Why? Where did they go? And where is God? What is He? I tried to squint, thinking that maybe I could make all the stars come back.

A quiet yearning rose up in me—and it was just then that I noticed that other "breathing" taking place in me. Perhaps it had been there all the time, ever since the millions of stars had ap-peared, but only now did it catch my attention.

I said to my father: "Can I ask you something, Dad?"

"What? About what?" he said, without turning his head. His voice was unusually calm.

"When Aunt Bertha died . . . when I was little . . . and we came back from the cemetery . . . do you remember what I asked you? And what you said?"

He did not immediately reply. I was asking him about the

death of his sister. There were six siblings in his family—five brothers and one sister, Bertha, the youngest of the children, beloved, and tenderly, protectively cherished by all the sons. When she was anywhere near the brothers they never shouted and almost never argued—even as a small child, I noticed that.

She was very beautiful; I have photographs of her that prove it to me, even now, many decades later. I have photographs of her holding my hand when I was just beginning to walk. In those pictures I can see in myself that absolute love and trust I felt for her all the days that she was with me.

She was nineteen years old when she was killed. She was struck by a car as she was crossing the wide street in front of the family house where we lived with my grandmother and all of her grown children. I could not have been much more than three years old. The words "Aunt Bertha is dead" had no meaning for me. I knew that bugs died, plants died, animals died. But I did not know what it meant that people died, especially people who were loved. When I heard those words coming from my father, with my mother weeping at his side, I became very still. Inside and outside. That is all.

My next intensely vivid memory is of the cemetery. I am standing next to my mother, who is holding my hand. It's a cold, sunny day. The coffin has just been lowered and is being covered with earth. The members of the family—many, many people— are standing listening to the rabbi as he chants in Hebrew while swaying back and forth, back and forth. My father and his four brothers, my uncles, are standing just behind the rabbi. In the middle, dressed—or I should say, covered—with black rags, supported at her elbows by the oldest son, Uncle Jack, and the next-to-oldest, my father, stands my grandmother.

It was startling to see her powerful, stout body trembling and weak, needing support, her face white with grief. Gray-black hair gushing as though electrified from under the loose black rags covering her head. I had already come to know her to be a kind of dragon, fierce eyes, fierce dark mole on her lip, her earthy Russian features with the high cheekbones that pressed upward into nearly Oriental eyes . . . served always by her angry sons who obeyed her every word, her every glance even as they shouted and roared at her. But now—how was it possible?—she could not even stand by herself; and yet—and how was this possible?—her weakness seemed in some way stronger than strength. I remember that I could not bear to look at her for more than a moment. I lowered my eyes.

And then, while my eyes are down, I am startled by noise and tumult and sudden movement all around. My mother suddenly, painfully, squeezes my hand and utters a groan. I remember being afraid to look up. And then—a surging need to know, to understand what is happening inside this unknown thing everyone called death and which I really did understand very deeply inside my child's bones and heart.

And when I do look up, I at first cannot make out what I am seeing. I see swirling black clouds at the grave and hear someone—I instantly know it is my grandmother—shrieking, screaming in the household Yiddish and Russian that I cannot understand. She has broken free from her sons and has leaped into the grave and is clawing at the earth even as it is still being shoveled onto the coffin.

It took all five of the brothers to tear her away from the coffin and lift her out of the grave. And it took all of them to hold her back, screaming at the open grave as the ceremony ended.

Back home in the big darkened house, furniture covered with white sheets. Shoes all left on the front porch. Everyone, like me, without shoes on. Seeing all the old people in their stocking feet somehow makes me feel that they are like me, a child. Mirrors and paintings all turned to the wall. The rabbi and the relatives being served tea and cakes by my mother and some of the other women. One of the old women, one of my great-aunts, offers me a small cake. The first time in my life anyone has "offered" me anything. People have *given* me things, but no one had ever *offered* me anything. It makes me now vaguely feel like a grown-up.

Soft, murmuring conversation. My grandmother, with two older women beside her, and holding a full glass of hot tea in her bare hand, sits staring and moaning on the couch. My father and the uncles are standing together, talking, in the enclosed, sunlit porch adjoining the darkened living room.

Independently, without asking anybody, I climb out of my slippery wooden chair and walk into the porch without anyone paying any attention to me.

I stand next to my father and feel absolutely no fear of him. I remember pulling at the sleeve of his coat. He looks down at me and says something like, "What do you want, Jerry?"

I vividly remember what I said, in a strong voice, tears streaming down my face:

"Where is Aunt Bertha?"

At that, the four uncles abruptly stopped talking and looked down at me.

My father looks into my face. He suddenly seems young, young and powerful, his eyes glistening:

"She's with God."

My words hang in the night air, "Do you remember?" But my father does not reply. He stays exactly as he was, his head tilted upward toward the sky.

But for me something important happened inside me. My mind started racing while at the same time my breathing became strangely quiet throughout my body. As a young child, from about the age of five onward, I had started precociously looking at books about astronomy, gradually becoming able actually to read and understand portions of the text. I started piling up information, facts about the solar system, the planets and the sun and the stars, devouring photographs, begging to be taken to the planetarium and, finally, talking endlessly about the universe and God with a special childhood friend. So just now, as I sat on the front steps with my father, my mind started racing with questions and thoughts about God and death. But there was something powerfully different about the present moment that made it unlike all my previous curiosity and questioning.

What made it different was that now, in the present moment, the memory of what I had felt at the death of my aunt and what I had felt tugging at the sleeve of my father—that memory was rising in my chest like the very power of darkest night itself. That memory wasn't really even a memory, it was a present experience, as present as the night sky, the lightning bugs, the sudden bursting sound of the loud crickets. What was present so powerfully at that moment was not a memory—that is too weak a word—it was my Self, it was what I was when I was three years old—what I was—no, *who* I was.

And *am*.

What I am saying is this:—and it is of utmost importance if any of us is ever to approach the question of what God is and what death is:

In that moment, sitting on the stone steps next to my silent father, I became two people: one thinking and questioning with all the information and logic at my disposal, and the other knowing and sensing and yearning within the depths of my embryonic and timeless Selfhood. And all the while there was no reconciling of these two human beings.

I tried as hard as I could to think. I formulated one question after another. Does God really exist? Why does He allow death and anguish? Why is He invisible? Why does He allow evil people to exist and make war and kill millions of innocent people? My mind raced through the books I was reading: astronomy, philosophy, biology, prehistory. The human mind—was God the Mind of the universe? And is the universe infinite? What could that mean? Is the human mind also infinite? . . . Or was it all—God and religion and ceremonies—all irrational? Something, beliefs, fairy tales or something, for someone else, for other people—not for me, not for science, not for philosophy.

As I tried and tried to pursue the thoughts that were endlessly erupting inside my skull, and as I tried to concentrate on them, I was also deeply aware—wordlessly—of the yearning and the vibration inside my chest, and the sensation of *I am* that had accompanied the millions of stars and the remembering of the death of Aunt Bertha.

The more I tried to think, the more I became aware of the wordless vibration in my body, the more I felt like two people—and the more I felt something like a second breathing taking place inside me. And the more acute became the sensation of being two separate people.

What I wish to say in this introductory chapter, what I wish to propose, is that when a man or woman directs his or her attention to questions of ultimate reality—which are in their essence the question of the nature of God—something awakens within us and calls to us; when a man or woman directs his or her attention to questions of ultimate value and ultimate obligation—which also are in their essence the question of the nature of God and God's need of us—something within us awakens and calls to us. That awakening something has no interest in material, worldly needs and attractions; no interest in pleasure or success or money or being first. I am calling it the soul (or the Self) for lack of a better word. It is not interested in what the *me* wants. It wishes only to live and grow and be.

The point here is that in childhood this soul, or Self, sometimes calls to us in resounding tones; or in front of death it often calls to us in resounding tones. But as we grow older and begin to be drawn into our place in the world around us, and if there are few or no influences to help us remember this soul or Self, if every time ultimate questions arise in our hearts and minds—as they inevitably do in childhood and as we grow older—if every time such questions arise in us, we are immediately pushed into solving, explaining, utilizing, winning, worrying, selling, needing to score or get it right, fighting off foolish materialism or foolish fundamentalism, itching to make our mark, or solve some intractable problem of human society, or pass a test, or persuade someone, or persuade many someones, or persuade the entire world, or become famous, or become a star or a guru, or, finally, give our precious free attention to more "realistic" questions of "real life,"—if, I say, we are rendered heedless with our precious little free attention and compelled to allow that precious little to be swallowed by the conditioned impulses and reactions of our egoism, then we will never come to an understanding of what God is. To understand what God is, to begin to understand what God is, demands from the very outset the presence in ourselves of what God is. I mean to say that God—or whatever we call essential reality—must already be active within our awareness when we turn to think about God.

Perhaps a better way to put this is to say that, if we look and observe ourselves, we will discover that the presence of a higher vibration within ourselves is already there, activating the impulse to think about the question of God. But we are all too often insensitive to this inner vibration from within the heart of man, from within the embryonic soul in which there circulates what may be called the "blood of God."

It does not matter whether we deny or affirm the existence of what the conventional world calls God. What matters is only that we are deeply and authentically concerned with questions of ultimate reality and ultimate value. It only matters that we are called to try to be honest and deep and good in our thought and life. We may come to the conclusion, as did Freud[1] and as do many others of us, that the world is laboring under illusions about God, and that these illusions are poisonous and dangerous to the whole life of man. That does not matter. What matters is this dual existence, this simultaneous existence in oneself of two natures, two nearly equal and honorable impulses: the love of Truth and the Good, and at the same time, the impulse to think critically, logically, and/or the impulse to behave effectively and under the rule of conscience in the world we live in and facing the people we are obliged, by all that is real, to help and care for.

I am saying that if we lose all contact with this inner God-element in ourselves—or, if you wish, call it our inner, wordless yearning to serve the Good and know the Truth—if we lose contact with this inner vibration, our thought and our action in the world will take us nowhere. Our thought will lead us either to cynicism or to an absurd overestimation of our mental powers. It will lead us to develop, in an onrushing torrent, inventions in the mind or in the physical world—ideologies or technologies—that, walled off from the impulse toward conscience and truth, can destroy us and our earth. On the other hand, if we lose all contact and respect for the powers and functions of our socially conditioned self, which is also given to us in order that we may become the instruments of love in the widening world of human beings and the world of nature—the world of nature which needs us to become fully human in order itself to serve the universal Good as a planet infused with human consciousness—if we lose all contact with this "horizontal" half of our human nature; if we unconsciously retreat into self-centered mysticism or self-willed, blind "faith," we may become like the "gods" of the Tibetan Buddhist teaching who, while possessed of higher energies, ultimately rot and suffer more than any other created being in the universe, and who create more evil and harm than any other force in the universe.

It was fortunate for me that there on the stone steps, my father remained silent. It enabled me to see more clearly this great division within myself between the eager, thinking, explaining mind and the vibration of the inner being. And it enabled me to see what I am calling the "breathing" of the soul. Years later, I came to see that there was obviously, and right in front of my eyes, something else—namely, a third something that was actually seeing this division—a third and finer attention, fragile and subtle, which later was to assume the proportions of an immense, unknown central question in my life and in my understanding.

But after having become aware of this strange, intimate twoness within myself, I began to be acutely aware of its presence or absence whenever I began to think about ultimate questions—and I engaged in such attempts to think very, very frequently as I was growing up, as do many of us, sometimes especially in our adolescence. And as time went on, and I began to be intentionally aware, even if only slightly, of my state of being when I tried to think about God or ultimate questions, I observed—at first vaguely, but eventually quite clearly—that when I thought about God or ultimate reality without any sense of the inner vibration of my being, then my thought simply raced ahead into complications and "ingenuity" without end or without substance. I became "clever" or "brilliant" or "imaginative." And I pushed hard to be "right," or "original," or "bold," or "up-to-date," etc. I received "recognition," and chose my friends accordingly, honing my ability to argue and score intellectual points.

But when that special yearning and vibration for a moment surfaced in my heart and body, even faintly, I experienced a despair about all my clever ideas: my philosophical success tasted bitter and empty; my conscience brought me the pain of remorse, which for years I reacted to with fits of depression in order to cover it over with self-pity or ever more fantastic dreams about my intrinsic worth and mental ability. And when, without knowing exactly what I was seeing, I saw in many of my valued friends and teachers this same heartless brilliance and cleverness, it served to increase my despair and cynicism about Truth and the Good.

More and more, as I see it now, this heartless way of thinking about God and ultimate reality dominates the mind of the contemporary world. For God or against God, "belief" or "atheism," it makes no difference unless the inner yearning—or whatever we wish to call the cause and source of the "second breathing"— is there. And it can so easily be there, just as it can so easily be covered over and ignored, perhaps for the rest of one's life. God or not God, "belief" or "science"—it also makes no real difference for my personal life unless the call of the Self and its need to "breathe" is heard and, ultimately, respected. Not only can thought about ultimate reality make no difference to the world or to my personal life unless we hear and respect the call of the Self, but such empty thought can bring down our personal and collective world, even our Earth itself. When thought races ahead of Being, a civilization is racing toward destruction.

CHAPTER TWO

Who Am I?

I became an atheist. The religion of my childhood, the religion of grandmothers and grandfathers and uncles and aunts and unknowable language and tedious chanting and arid holidays, had nothing to do with the sky full of stars, the still and silent mantis, or the surging water of the Wissahickon Creek. It had nothing to do with what early in my life, from my father, I had learned to call God.

On my father's side of the family, away from his hidden inner life, God was a severe and punitive tyrant. On my mother's side, God was a just but distant king. A king who allowed His people the warmth and loving care for each other that my mother embodied in her daily life, who allowed His people joyful feasts and banter and the glad duty of familial forgiveness. But although that element of my childhood brought me a precious measure of security and happiness, and in a sense probably saved my life, I felt in it no more connection to what I felt to be God than I did to the tyrant God.

As my education led me more and more into the study of nature and philosophical reasoning, I even refused to think that word, "God." Nature, life in all its awesome beauty and purpose, was simply and purely *what is*. It was simply and purely *the way things are*. And that was quite enough for me. That was god enough for me. I had no way of knowing or suspecting that in taking this turn of mind, I was taking a real step toward understanding what God actually is, toward understanding what it even means to understand that word to which I had now become allergic.

A Carefully Chosen Question

And here I am, on New York's Upper West Side in the spring of 1957, twenty-two years old, sitting stiffly on an ornate armless chair outside the living room of a man who I had come to suspect was something like a genuine Zen master—whatever that was. That man was the renowned Japanese scholar D. T. Suzuki.

In my last year at college, at Harvard, I had been devouring a just-published paperback book titled simply *Zen Buddhism,* consisting of a handful of Suzuki's essays written to introduce Zen to the Western world. And this it did, to an extent few could have foreseen.

Now, a half-century later, "Zen" seems to be everywhere. Toward one end of a very broad spectrum, serious Zen Buddhist spiritual communities are to be found throughout America and Europe, and, beyond that, many thousands of men and women throughout the Western world have become eager students of

Zen Buddhist writings and teachings. But also, toward the other end of the spectrum—with many gradations of seriousness and banality in between—the once vitally incomprehensible language of Zen has become intellectually and even commercially *fashionable*. The Zen word "satori," for example, which refers to the inexpressible experience of awakening from all egoistic self-illusions, now is widely used on such things as perfumes, tanning lotions and corporate logos. A similar fate has befallen the Zen word "koan." Koans are spiritual exercises in the form of profoundly irrational or paradoxical questions. Within one of the branches of the Zen Buddhist tradition (the Rinzai school), these logically unanswerable questions are employed with surgical precision—always within the rigorous conditions of the traditional master-pupil relationship—as an instrument, or "skillful means," the purpose of which is to repeatedly shock the pupil as part of a long and difficult struggle: the struggle to free himself from the intellect's posture as interpreter and defender of one's own self-identity. When Zen was first entering the West, the word had tremendous energy and mystery, and brought a tremendous challenge to the vaunted "rational" mind. At the present time in the West, however, the word "koan" and the idea of the practice associated with it has lost almost all of the healthy shock value it once had. Koans? Yes, of course I know what they are! "What is the sound of one hand clapping?" Oh yes, fascinating. And even very amusing.

But in 1957, to the philosophy graduate student anxiously waiting to encounter the Zen man himself, everything about

Zen Buddhism was filled with amazement and wonder. And hope. But what kind of hope was this that took the form of incomprehensible ideas magically expressed in simple, gentle, yet dramatic terms that seemed to deny the very essence of rational thought? What kind of hope was it that took the form of teachers who taught not by words or logic or analysis or philosophical insight, but by shouts and silences and rude (but mysteriously benign) actions?

And what would the Zen man say or do to me when I was finally invited into the room behind the closed French doors? I had armed myself with a carefully chosen question to put to him, a question that had just been the subject of my senior-year philosophy dissertation: "What is the Self?" Into that lengthy dissertation I had poured all my latest intellectual passions, stirring them together into some kind of indigestible, metaphysical soup. In that soup were large pieces of Kierkegaard, fragments of Heidegger, slivers of Kant and Vedanta along with now personally embarrassing borrowings from the Zen man, D. T. Suzuki himself, whom I was about to meet. My professor at the time, the kindly existentialist philosopher John Wild, had given me a good grade, possibly to encourage me to go on studying these writings until I actually understood something about them.

Or at least until I might come to realize that I had understood very little indeed. I had taken the great nineteenth-century spiritual philosopher Søren Kierkegaard and, without any pangs of conscience, had enthusiastically stripped the religious dimension from his books, imagining that the inferno of his inner life and self-confrontation, transcending all logic and systematic thought, could be embraced without any reference at all to his relationship to God, to what on almost every page he also calls "the eternal." I had no idea that everything he was writing—his incomparable poetic and literary genius, his stunningly flesh-and-blood philosophical arguments and attacks—were modeled on what he felt in his heart about the essential nature of divine revelation. The "eternal," for Kierkegaard—perhaps we may also call it the "higher"—comes toward man through a paradoxical fusion of pure gift from Above and radical inner choice from within; that is, from the total freedom of inwardly sacrificing all of one's hopes and self-identity in the specifically human act of submission to the eternal, an act that Kierkegaard called *the leap of faith.* Specifically human because to be human is to be, as Kierkegaard understood it, a paradoxical inner reconciliation of two opposing realities: the eternal and the temporal, the infinite and the finite. How could I have imagined otherwise? How could I have seen his writings as a celebration of empty freedom devoid of all foundation in an openness to God? I wasn't alone in this misunderstanding, of course. Much of twentieth-century existentialist philosophy, including the stirring work of Jean-Paul Sartre, was rooted in this misunderstanding of Kierkegaard. Through the existentialists, Kierkegaard's depiction of the limit-less freedom of mankind that is concealed under all the condi-tioning of our biology and social conventions—his depiction of this wondrous and terrifying freedom—served as a magnet for an entire generation of questioning men and women who sought to affirm the cosmic uniqueness of man without being bullied by scientific materialism on the one hand and dogmatic, conventional religious concepts of God on the other hand. How were any of us really to know that without God, Kierkegaard's writings were meaningless—just as, so he taught, without God there was, in fact, no such thing as freedom and, in fact, no such thing as human life itself?

And how was I possibly to understand his contradictions and paradoxes, his literary thunderbolts, his winding novelistic psychological ascents and descents—how was I to understand that all his "answers" were inevitably swallowed by ever deepening questions? How was I to understand that the form of his work was intentionally designed to point me toward finding the answer not only for myself, but *in* myself and not on the printed page or in the abstract words of an author? Kierkegaard called this method of writing *indirect communication*, and in it he mimicked, so he was telling us, how God Himself, the Eternal itself, revealed Truth to man. How was this graduate student in philosophy to understand all this that went against the rational, systematic and scientific brilliance of the modern Western mind?—while at the same time this graduate student was drawn more and more toward a great *Something* in Kierkegaard, *Something* wearing the skin-tight garment of paradox and "irrationality"? Had not Kierkegaard written such things as: "A direct relationship between one spiritual being and another, with respect to the essential truth, is unthinkable. If such a relationship is assumed, it means that one of the parties has ceased to be spirit"? Had he not also written: "It would mean very little if one persuaded millions of men to accept the truth, if precisely by the method of their acceptance they were transferred into error"?[2] It sounded wondrous to me, but I did not understand it at all— and I did not know that I did not understand it.

And had not Kierkegaard also written about my Socrates, my personal "god": "Socrates was an ethical teacher, but he took cognizance of the non-existence of any direct relationship between the teacher and the pupil, because the truth is inwardness, and because this inwardness in each is precisely the road which leads them [the teacher and the pupil] away from one another . . . [because] the inwardness of the truth is not the comradely inwardness with which two bosom friends walk arm in arm, but the separation with which each for himself exists in truth."[3] I loved such statements and I imagined I understood what Kierkegaard meant by "inwardness." In fact, I did not understand it at all. But it called to me; Lord, how it called to me!

I heard movement behind the closed doors and I tried to pull myself together. A nice-looking Japanese woman opened the door and said that Dr. Suzuki would see me now.

The next thing I remember is not the size or shape of the room, nor the furnishings, nor the lighting, nor the kind of chair I sat in. I remember only the face and figure of Suzuki himself— especially the eyebrows, which seemed to grow out from his forehead like enormous wings. He was old, slightly built like most Japanese; I vaguely remember a cardigan sweater and a bow tie. But what I do remember very clearly was his *presence*.

My mind went blank. The sight of him instantly went right through my armor. Strangely—although, in the light of the laws of man's inner life, not so strangely—my feeling of nervousness was for a brief few moments nothing more than a leaf in the wind. For a few moments I was simply a naked mind—neither anxious nor confident. Looking back on that unforgettable moment, I see now that I—that is, my mental attention—had for a fleeting moment, and to a certain extent, withdrawn from my thoughts and fears and had descended into the whole of my body. But it has taken me many years to understand that this is in fact what had happened to me, and to realize that it was this diffusion of the attention of the mind into the whole body that was what Suzuki had been describing in most of his books, and especially in his essay "Zen and Swordsmanship," which for me had been among the most riveting of his writings.

In that essay he cites a letter written by the Zen master Takuan (1573–1645) concerning the relationship between Zen and the art of swordsmanship:

> *The thing is . . . to let it [the mind] fill up the whole body, let it flow throughout the totality of your being. When this happens you use the hands when they are needed, you use the legs or the eyes when they are needed, and no time or extra energy will be wasted. . . When the mind fills up the*

body entirely, it is said to be right . . . The right mind is
equally distributed over the body . . . The mind is not to be
treated like a cat tied to a string. The mind must be left to
itself, utterly free to move about according to its own
nature. Not to localize or partialize it is the end of spiritual
training. When it is nowhere it is everywhere. When it
occupies one tenth, it is absent in the other nine tenths. Let
the swordsman discipline himself to have the mind go on
its own way, instead of deliberately trying to confine it
somewhere.[4]

However, the moment I began to speak to Dr. Suzuki all my attention rushed back up from my body into my head, which started to spin round and around with words, searching for something appropriate to say. Being still young, and very much stuffed with academic forms of thought, I did not even notice this change of state as such—and Dr. Suzuki's silence did not help me to understand what was happening in me. Not then, in any case. But only later. Quite a bit later.

I do not remember anything I said during the next ten minutes or so, except for some vague remarks about the Gurdjieff teaching, which I had begun studying a few months before, but without staying with it. I had heard that Suzuki had had contact with some of the teachers in that tradition and I asked him what he thought of it. He said simply that he did not understand what they were trying. That took me aback, but it also gave me the impetus to ask the one question that I had been carefully guarding and that I was sure would open up a challenging discussion with Dr. Suzuki, as well as showing him how serious a thinker I was and how well I understood what was, in general, important.

"What is the self?" I said.

I prepared myself to listen very carefully to his reply in order to carry the discussion further. Crowding the front of my brain, like devoted servants eagerly waiting to be called down to my lips, were Kierkegaard, Heidegger, Socrates, Immanuel Kant and many others.

He smiled slightly with the left side of his mouth; and his bat-wing eyebrows twitched.

"Who is asking the question?"

I looked at him, dumbfounded. Of course, I ought to have been well prepared for such a question. Had I not read hundreds of accounts of just such a question being put by this or that Zen master to one or another monk? But it was suddenly as though I had never read a single book about Zen or even heard of it. As for my good servants Kierkegaard, Heidegger, Socrates, Kant and all their company, they bolted away from the front of my mind like startled birds frightened by a gunshot.

"*I* am asking it!" I stammered like a fool, even with a shade of annoyance.

"Show me this *I*," he said.

Never had I felt more helpless. What the hell was he talking about? In fact, I actually felt a bit insulted.

"What do you mean?"

But he said nothing more. He simply sat there, silent, courteous, serious. As though there was nothing at all strange about this conversation.

And I could think of nothing more to say, nothing at all.

Minutes passed, agonizingly. Silence suffocated me.

Eventually, the Japanese woman brought in a tray of tea, and I remember that I did manage to stay a few minutes longer and carry on a conversation. But I have no idea what we spoke about or even how I got out the door.

I was deeply disappointed. On the train back to New Haven I could think of nothing else but my disappointment.

A Tiger Does Not Withdraw

Months passed. I worked hard at my studies: metaphysics, the dialogues of Plato, the American philosophical tradition of pragmatism and common sense. But I was repeatedly haunted by my disappointment with Suzuki. I was even in the midst of an intensive seminar concerning the history of Zen Buddhism—taught by the eminent Buddhist scholar Johannes Rahder. But although I read massive amounts of Zen Buddhist texts and scholarly analyses, they did not in the least ease the emptiness I felt over that encounter with Suzuki. Never did it enter my head that he had given me a gift—and that now something was in some way up to me. I felt only—vaguely—that my last chance at entering something both fundamentally real and fundamentally sacred had been taken away from me. Without naming it as such, I felt totally adrift—not, as the existentialists would say, adrift in the universe, but adrift within myself. Gurdjieff had been a great hope of sorts, but now that was gone; Zen Buddhism and Suzuki were now also gone. And the harder I worked at my academic studies, the emptier they felt, an emptiness I tried to fill up with the craving for intellectual brilliance.

I cultivated friendships with fellow students, several of whom were soon to become giants in their fields—an exquisitely gifted poet, a towering master of English literature, a uniquely original and uniquely challenging analytic philosopher, and a greatly gifted historian and synthesizer of modern philosophical trends. Endless conversations where I tried to hold my own with these immensely gifted minds while at the same time—unbeknownst to my ego, my "I," my fragile sense of identity—fighting for the existence of God and the sacred. Unbeknownst to me, the question of who I was and the question of who or what God was—this was the same question! And, let me now say, this *is* the same question—but not at all in any self-inflating sense, or sentimentally understood "mystical" sense; or in any existentially sad and lonely sense of the poor human consciousness adrift in a blind, mechanical universe. And even as I write this, I glimpse in myself the real energy of the question *Who am I*, and its identity with the question of what God is, slipping away under the surface of my awareness.

It withdraws, this question and this identity—it withdraws from awareness. It is a tiger, this question, and while a tiger does not withdraw, I myself withdraw from it. You cannot play intellectual games with this tiger—or rather, that is all you can do, that is all I could do at that time in my life. I came to many great insights about the union of self and Self. Insights about the greatness of the traditions of India and the fundamental doctrine of *Atman* and *Brahman*—the great Self within man and the great Self of the universe. I wrote excellent philosophical papers, even making what I believed were important discoveries about the underlying correspondence between Buddhism, which denies the reality of the self, and Hinduism, which emphasizes the ultimate reality of what is also called the "self." As for Judaism, and of course even more so with what very little I understood or even wanted to understand about Christianity—well, they were long gone in my mind. Gone. Irrelevant.

It seemed that I had been able to put Suzuki and my disappointment out of my mind. After all, what was one more disappointment in a life that wasn't really going anywhere other than being an express train to academic success and the establishment of originality and influence and recognition and . . . despair? Under it all, nearly always, there was this faint bitter taste.

It was sometime toward the very end of my first year as a graduate student at Yale, several months after my meeting with D. T. Suzuki. I was living in a small rented room a few blocks away from the campus. In the middle of the night, in the middle of a sound sleep, I suddenly sat bolt upright in bed.

My God! This was what he was telling me! It was all intentional on his part! I was supposed to find this out by myself! It was not communicable in words, in thought! It was an event, not an idea! Who am I? This state was the answer!

But amazing to me as this was, the most amazing thing was the fact that such "indirect communication"[5] actually existed. I was stunned and deeply joyous that there was such a thing as what Kierkegaard called the communication between man and man—communication not of results, but of the discovery of awakening—or something like that. And I was joyously aware that in this miraculous communication there was a quality of— yes, the word is correct—there was a quality of love—and a quality of respect that I had never before experienced in my life. Yes, the words are right, but I did not use those words to myself at that time. I understood the rightness of this word, love, only later from the teachers who were to enter my life in the future and far away from where I was then. But it was love, it was respect, it was the action of one who looked at me, and no doubt at all human beings, as essentially awakened consciousness, and not as the ego I felt myself to be.

And not only would it gradually become clear to me that the question What is God? is the same question as Who am I? but something else would become clear, something that I never imagined I would even take seriously. The phrase, "God is love," had always seemed fairylike and sentimental and, well, incomprehensible. Dimly, without my knowing it then, sitting up in my bed in the middle of the night, I was stepping through a door onto a long road that led to the direct understanding of this most mysterious and unfathomable and yet obvious definition of the word God: God is love. It would be many years until that experiential seed would begin to push through into my consciousness and my search for meaning.

CHAPTER THREE

God and the Mind

The course was called "The History of Western Religious Thought," and even after three years I still couldn't believe I was actually teaching it. Looking back now, more than forty years later, I thank fate, or accident, with the whole of my being for putting me into this impossible situation.

In 1962, in desperate need of an academic job and having nowhere else to turn, I inquired about an opening in the philosophy department in what was then a remote and professionally unglamorous San Francisco State College, far away and far down the cultural ladder from the ivy-covered walls of the East Coast academic establishment. At that time, as I recall, because of its founding charter, the college required that such a course be provided for students intending to enter the clergy. And so, in order to be considered for this position an applicant had to teach a course which in those days (and to a great extent even now) almost no so-called "mainstream" philosopher would touch with a ten-foot or even twenty-foot pole—namely, the history of Jewish and Christian thought. In applying for this position, I may have been the only candidate willing to take on the task of preparing and teaching such a course. In any case, I got the job.

In those days, and, as I say, to a great extent even now, mainstream academic philosophy was constitutionally incapable and unwilling to take seriously or even to perceive the intellectual content of religion. It is true that philosophers did deal with a subject which they called "the philosophy of religion." But this marginal branch of professional philosophy consisted mainly of logical, critical analysis from the outside, centering almost entirely on only one element of religion, "faith," which was taken to mean little more than blind, unjustified belief. That religion at its root is also a great work of the mind was nowhere even imagined. That Judaism or Christianity offers ideas of immense sophistication and power about reality, man, nature, history, art, and the whole theater of human life—this was nowhere even imagined in the mainstream of academic philosophy.

For me to be now giving a course about Judaism, just that Judaism which I had run away from without ever looking back—that was strange enough. But to be standing in front of a college-level class and teaching an in-depth, year-long course also about Christianity—that was truly unbelievable.

About Judaism I had known only what I had automatically absorbed by ethnic, familial osmosis, and by a few weeks in my sophomore year at college studying one or two Old Testament selections in a required introductory humanities course.

And as for Christianity, it is no mere figure of speech to say that I understood less than nothing. I entered that introductory humanities course hating and fearing Christianity. During my childhood years I had watched my father humiliated and cheated in business by people who called themselves "Christians." And I myself, walking home from school, had to be continually on guard against the tough Catholic kids who were always out to get the neighborhood kike.

In that same humanities course we were also obliged to read portions of the New Testament—the pages of which I could hardly even bear to touch. It is probably impossible to communicate the revulsion toward Jesus that was commonly felt by most Jews in families like my own. Even to speak his name would have been an outrage within the walls of our home. Hadn't we been butchered and tortured and reviled across the world and throughout history by the followers of this "Jesus" and his gospel of love? However, I did manage to read through the class assignments— parts of Matthew, the beginning chapters of John, and Paul's Epistles to the Romans and Corinthians. And, with the help of what we called a "pony"—these were short, handy booklets neatly summarizing various college texts—I was able to fight my way through the first midterm exam.

But when it came to *The Confessions of St. Augustine*, I was utterly defeated. Our assignment was to read not just one or two excerpts, but the entire book. And I could hardly even make it through the first paragraph:

Great art Thou, O Lord, and greatly to be praised; great is Thy power and Thy wisdom infinite. And Thee would

man praise; man, but a particle of Thy creation; man, that
bears about him his mortality, the witness of his sin, the
witness that "Thou resistest the proud": yet would man
praise Thee; he, but a particle of Thy creation. Thou
awakest us to delight in Thy praise: for Thou madest us for
Thyself, and our heart is restless until it repose in Thee[6] ...
et cetera, et cetera, et cetera ...

It wasn't simply that I found this sort of thing difficult to follow;
I could not even want to follow it. It was like poison to me. Not
the least of the problems were the thous and thees, which in a
pinch I could accept in the Bible, just because it was, well, the
Bible—an ancient, "hallowed" text supposedly authorized by an
incomprehensible God Himself and therefore legitimately em-
ploying more or less incomprehensible language.

But far more offensive to me was what my sophomore
mind took to be the obsequious *Christian-ness* of Saint Augustine. What was all this bowing and scraping? What was all this
self-deprecation? What was all this whining and pleading? All
this—and this word blinded me more than anything else—all
this *sin*.

There at the beginning and on every page thereafter, in
every paragraph and, it seemed, every sentence—there was this
sin. It seemed that poor Mister Saint Augustine could not even
take a breath or eat an apple, far less perform any normal, meaningful human interaction with other human beings or the world

around him, without drenching it in his sin and guilt. Even to the point of pitifully confessing his sin as a newborn infant sucking at his mother's breast! Even to the point of wondering if he had been absorbed in sin when still in the womb! And all the while thanking this all-good, all-merciful God . . . for what? No, all this was more than I could bear.

And this went on and on, through infancy, boyhood, and—God forbid!—adolescence, when sexual energy begins to arise as it does in any normal human child. And, to complete the picture, this universally acclaimed world-famous titanic mind, full of the most intricate philosophical lines of argument and questioning—philosophical reasoning of great power that I should have been able to respectfully study—philosophical examinations of supposedly great depth about the mind, time, symbolism, memory, the theory of knowledge and more—even in the midst of streams and streams of complex, subtle thought, here was this insufferable, guilt-ridden, Christ-ridden, self-abasing Christian soaking all this philosophy in thous and thees and sin, sin, sin, and unjustifiable, hypocritical gratitude to the God who created him just as he was. I could not and would not and did not understand or wish to understand, or even acknowledge, the mind of this Christian Saint Augustine. Every time I tried to read the text I would start dreaming of the last day of class when I would immediately throw the book into a fire that I would kindle for just this purpose in the fireplace of the rather elegant Harvard College dormitory living quarters that I shared with two other students who, like me, were bound for careers in science and medicine, far, far away from anything that smelled of religion or the God of religion.

And, in fact, on the very day of the final examination, one hour afterward, I did just what I had dreamed of—lighting a fire and very, very slowly burning the book, one horrible page at a time, staring with great satisfaction at all the thous and thees and sins blackening and disappearing up the chimney into the cold, dark December air.

And yet: Here I was teaching about Christianity! And what was one of my texts? Nothing other than *The Confessions of St. Augustine*! Was it forced upon me? Was it a text required by the department curriculum committee? Not at all; I had willingly, eagerly, chosen it—because, in fact, in preparing myself three years before to teach this course, I had reluctantly picked up the book and was deeply moved by its power.

Having said (or should I say, "confessed") all this, I wish to allow the simple fact of my turnabout involving Saint Augustine to serve just now only as a springboard for speaking about the vast depths of ideas and thought that I began to discover in Judaism and Christianity, depths that are still hidden from many people who are, as I was, unable to see beneath the surface of our culture's religious symbols and doctrines. Even now, after so many years devoted to the theoretical and practical study of religious thought, I see again and again, time after time, that what I have taken to be the deeper meaning of the Judaic and Christian idea of God is only another "surface"—however deep, relatively, it may lie—behind or beneath which, or within which, the real mystery of the meaning of God still remains hidden in all its unformed and unmanifested power.

A New Judaism

Starting, then, with Judaism:

Months before I was to start teaching the course, I rolled up my sleeves and promised myself that I would set aside all my adolescent religious allergies in order genuinely and respectfully to inform myself about the ideas and practices of the religion of my childhood, about which I knew shamefully little. I read and studied many books, some by well-known popular authors (such as Herman Wouk's *This Is My God*) and many others by highly regarded, established Jewish and non-Jewish scholars and theologians. But, late in August of that year, 1962, driving across America in my battered yellow Chevrolet—and scheduled to arrive in San Francisco a mere ten days before the beginning of the semester—I felt still utterly unprepared to teach the class. I mean to say that nothing in all the material I had read had touched my heart. Or, what was even more troubling, my mind.

Yes, I was now ready to lecture honorably about many of the main concepts of the tradition: about monotheism, which we Jews supposedly invented; about the admonitions and teachings of the prophets and the Hebraic idea of God acting in history; about the primacy of the ethical dimension in Judaism; about the idea of idolatry, about the creation of the world and Man . . . And yes, I was prepared to squeeze out from the Old Testament recognizable philosophical issues relating to established academic branches of philosophy—issues dealing with epistemology (the theory of knowledge), metaphysics (the nature of reality) and, of course, ethics, But it was all so empty, so fundamentally irrelevant to the drama of living, suffering, loving, dying . . . .

Because a man lived, suffered, loved and died alone, in his own blood-red living skin, without hollow concepts and dried-out intellectual problems to muffle his cries and shouts and exultations. Yes, I now had some good, established conceptual accounts of Judaism, which I had never known or imagined to exist when I was younger. But they added nothing at all to my feeling for Judaism. On the contrary.

And how could it have been otherwise? These words—God, duty, commandment, creation, good and evil—had become an essential, fundamental part of the nervous system of Western civilization, just that Western civilization which had ultimately become hellishly meaningless and hellishly lonely. It was words like these which had become the main instrument of my own, and almost everyone's, modern mind; the main instruments of perception, thinking, judgment, questioning. So common and everyday had these words become, so abstract, so empty, so indefinable, or rather so multi-definable, so lending themselves to fatuous metaphysical speculation or fantastic ramblings, self-deceptive insights, going round and round, like strange neon lights guiding us into dark alleys and dismal encounters and empty philosophical ambitions that were dead and refuted the moment they were realized. No wonder I, personally, could go only to nature and to the wild, or to the brave existentialists; no wonder the spiritual mind was showing itself in our world only in the wonders of what began as pure, nonmaterialistic science on the one hand, and on the other hand, what continually erupted as the attempted creation of new language—in poetry, in music, in dangerous art, or, lately—in that deep, strange and strangely hopeful Zen Buddhism and, maybe a little, a precious little, in the mysticism of India—*maybe*.

Judaism? If the purpose of a religion was to lead man away from emptiness into real meaningful human-ness, then Judaism ought to be offering humanity an escape from, freedom from—from what? From Judaism itself!

I did my professional best, but I could not blame my students if so many of them may have been bored or confused by my dutiful attempts to make the Old Testament philosophically interesting. The academic year ended. During the summer, moving into new living quarters and unpacking boxes of books that until then had been in storage, my eyes fell upon a book called *Major Trends in Jewish Mysticism*. It was one of dozens of books about Judaism and Christianity that I had feverishly bought months before leaving for California when I was searching for something, anything, to help me prepare to teach the class.

I had no idea why I had bought that book; I didn't even remember buying it. If there was anything in the world that was more distasteful or uninteresting to me than what I had known to be Judaism, it was, hands down, "mysticism." To me the word called to mind only some special kind of experience rooted perhaps in sexual neurosis, which self-deluded men and women of the past and present claimed gave them direct contact with what they called "God," or the "Absolute," or some such "ultimate reality." The mystic never tired of saying that what he or she had experienced was "ineffable," impossible to describe or communicate, but that at the same time it held the key to all the mysteries and questions of human life. And we poor mortals were supposed to take their word for it? We poor mortals with our pathetic Einstein, Newton, Plato, Immanuel Kant, Kierkegaard; our mere Shakespeare or Dostoyevsky; our little Nietzsche or Freud; or our pitiful Johann Sebastian Bach, Mozart or Beethoven. These "mystics" had gone beyond these towering giants? What nonsense!

Why would I have bought a book with a title like that? Judaism itself or mysticism itself was difficult enough for me to swallow. But Judaism and mysticism *together*? What was I thinking?

Standing there, surrounded by shelves and floor space chaotically piled up with unpacked books, I idly began thumbing through that thick paperback book, and almost against my will, my attention was caught by one passage after another:

> *Language in its purest form, that is, Hebrew, according to the Kabbalists, reflects the spiritual nature of the world; in other words, it has a mystical value. Speech reaches God because it comes from God.*[7]

Hmmm . . .

> *The mystics, too, speak of creation out of nothing; in fact, it is one of their favorite formulae. But in their case the orthodoxy of the term conceals a meaning which differs considerably from the original one. This Nothing from which everything has sprung is by no means a mere negation; only to us does it present no attributes because it is beyond the reach of intellectual knowledge. In truth, however, this Nothing . . . is infinitely more real than all other reality. Only when the soul has stripped itself of all limitation and, in mystical language, has descended into the depths of Nothing does it encounter the Divine . . .*[8]

Interesting . . . is this really Judaism? Sounds like . . . what?

> *The prophetic faculty, according to this doctrine, represents the union of the human intellect at the highest stage of its*

development, with a cosmic influence normally domiciled in the intelligible world, the so-called active intellect (intellectus agens). The influx of this active intellect into the soul manifests itself as prophetic vision.[9]

Head down, my attention buried in the book, I absently walked over to a rocking chair facing the bay window of my tiny new apartment and sat down. My hand by itself reached up and found the switch on a standing lamp even though there was still plenty of afternoon light.

I continued flipping through the book, slowly devouring whole pages at a time, and again and again being brought to a sudden stop when my mind could take no more and had to try to rearrange the elements of its understanding of Judaism—and even of religion itself.

So! The God of Judaism was not some naïve anthropomorphic projection, nor was He a mere poetic metaphor at the heart of some all-too-human conflicted narrative. Not at all. Here was a God radiating immense cosmic forces as inescapable as any scientific laws, but as full of wordless purpose and meaning as divine music and heartbreaking love. *Here was the God of my father's sky!* And a God of animals and creatures of earth, a God of seeds, a God of storms and endless time. A God who needed Man!—and yet in Himself who remained as unknown and unknowable as birth and death themselves. This was no God of arbitrary rules and customs and meaningless musty rituals and tedious formulae. The moral demands emanating from this God were fused with the forces of creation itself, a creation, a universe, in which—just as my revered Plato had taught—Reality and Goodness were one; where Truth and Love were one; where right and wrong were not, ultimately, human inventions serving blind egoistic urges or fantasies, but were in fact forces of nature entwined around each other within the human psyche and within the dynamism of the moving life of the earth and the heavens.

What is this Reality? This universe? The world, the cosmos, the skies we see are aspects of a universe that is, as a whole, the manifestation of the intrinsically unknown God-Beyond-God. The universe is—in a profound sense of the term—the *expression* of God! No wonder it was called by some the *Logos*, the Word of God. What an idea! What a nest of ideas! How stupid I had been to grow up imagining that I knew what such words as "God" and "creation" meant. How stupid I must have imagined the ancient line of teachers to have been to believe such childish imaginings! I was now being engulfed in the world of ideas—and it was as though a powerful electric arc, crackling with life and energy, connected the religion of my childhood with the awesome and rational, philosophic beauty of Plato's dialogues and Socrates' subtle arguments for conscience, as well as with Kierkegaard's vibrant anxiety and passion and Nietzsche's sacred anger. And how arrogant I had been to judge so-called uneducated men and women who, yes, took the religion literally, but many of whom transformed the literal meanings with their whole-being-love and need for God, God the representation of the higher in human and earthly life. How arrogant and stupid to judge people whose quality of trust and faith towered far above my own puny logic and philosophical sleight of hand!

Night had fallen. Hours had passed. Joyously, I looked forward to the coming academic year and the course I had until then felt as a burden.

CHAPTER FOUR

God and the Mind II

But what about Christianity? What about Jesus? Would my unexpected turning toward Judaism open me to Christianity as
well? That possibility hovered near me in the days and weeks
that followed, as I immersed myself in Jewish texts and commentaries, mystical and otherwise.

A possibility, yes. But I could not yet give that possibility
my attention. I had become like the young boy looking up in
wonder at the night sky, looking at living nature, at the awesome phenomenon of the human body—at all of life. I was once
again being brought to tears by something far greater than myself which at the same time called forth everything in me that
yearned to think deeply and clearly. It was now as it was when I
was young: the more I was deeply silenced by what I was discovering, the more I felt driven to understand and know. The more
I learned in the books I was reading, the more I saw how little I
knew, or perhaps could ever know. And the more my respect
grew for this newly discovered Judaism.

How different this was from my early reactions to Judaism—
where the more I confronted a religion that could not be ratio-

nally explained, the more I lost respect and turned away. What was at the root of this entirely opposite relationship between the mind and that which was beyond the power of my mind to grasp? Why was I now feeling humbled where before I was self-assured and dismissive?

I am tempted to answer this question by citing yet more of the ideas that were now calling to me from the many books I was reading. Among these books was *The Zohar*[10]—that churning ocean of esoteric vision and wondrous spiritual interrogation which entered the Jewish tradition in medieval Spain. And there was the incomparable *Guide for the Perplexed*[11] by the great twelfth-century Jewish thinker Moses Maimonides, with its astonishing blend of philosophical precision, magisterial scholarship, and endlessly subtle psychological intuition and mystical insight.

And from our own time, there were also the writings of Martin Buber, especially his philosophical tone-poem, *I and Thou*.[12] I wrestled happily with that book's one great stroke of thought dividing all human relationship into I–Thou and I–It, an absolutely crucial distinction for a culture falling under the sway of science and technology, a distinction that allows modern people to find a clearly defined and respected place for both of the two necessary human worlds: the world of the soul and the world of the thing. And what a help it was, for someone like me, to begin to think of God as the eternal *Thou* rather than merely as an *It*—merely as an object among objects to be approached by heartless proofs and mental logic. This was my first glimpse—and it was only a glimpse—of the essence of Judaism as the demand and *pleading* from "above" to know God through the world of *Thou,* that is, through the work of love for man—not only man in general (which is sometimes possible), but the man or woman next to me, my neighbor (which is immensely difficult).

And then there was Buber's *Tales of the Hasidim.*[13]

In Eastern Europe, in the second half of the eighteenth century, a vibrant current of down-to-earth Jewish mysticism arose that was as rigorous as it was joyous. Founded by a certain Israel ben Eliezer, commonly known as the Baal Shem Tov ("the Master of the Good Name"), it spread among the common people of that part of the world through a powerful line of spiritual descendants of the founder. Countless stories, tales and anecdotes have been recorded illustrating the lightning-flash transmission from master to pupil of a moment of inner self-questioning and awakening, stories that resemble, in their concentration and mystery, accounts of the interaction of a Zen master and pupil. Buber collected many of these stories and retold them with literary skill and minimal explanation.

Now, here, with these two large volumes of Hasidic tales on my desk in front of me, I find it nearly impossible to recapture the impression they first made on me. I have lived with them on and off for the greater part of my life, and over the years, through some kind of magic, their meaning continually deepens and changes in a way that verifies whatever I have come to feel at the moment is most important in my own personal search. So, in this case, rather than try to find my way back beneath all the meanings that the years have layered over these stories, I wish simply to provide a few terse examples without comment. I only would say that it is in such anecdotal accounts that the answer lies to my personal question of why I began to respect rather than dismiss a Judaism which surpassed my mind's habit of seeking explanations. All I can or ought to say further about this is to call up an ancient saying—which comes from I don't remember where—to the effect that the only real proof of the existence of God is the existence of inwardly developed human beings—along with the existence in oneself of that which can recognize them.

A few brief anecdotes, then:

Before his death, Rabbi Zusya said, "In the coming world, they will not ask me: 'Why were you not Moses?' They will ask me: 'Why were you not Zusya?'" [14]

The disciples of the Baal Shem heard that a certain man had a great reputation for learning. Some of them wanted to go to him and find out what he had to teach. The master gave them permission to go, but first they asked him: "And how shall we be able to tell whether he is a true zaddik [holy man]?"

The Baal Shem replied, "Ask him to advise you what to do to keep unholy thoughts from disturbing you in your prayers and studies. If he gives you advice, then you will know that he belongs to those who are of no account. For this is the service of men in the world to the very hour of their death; to struggle time after time with the extraneous, and time after time to uplift and fit it into the nature of the Divine Name."[15]

[The Baal Shem said:] "Imagine a man whose business hounds him through many streets and across the market-place the livelong day. He almost forgets that there is a Maker of the world. Only when the time for the Afternoon Prayer comes, does he remember: 'I must pray.' And then, from the bottom of his heart, he heaves a sigh of regret that he has spent his day in vain and idle matters, and he runs into a by-street and stands there, and prays: God holds him dear, very dear and his prayer pierces the firmament."[16]

Once the Baal Shem summoned Sammael, lord of demons, because of some important matter. The Lord of demons roared at him: "How dare you summon me! Up to now this has happened to me only three times; in the hour at the Tree of Knowledge, the hour of the golden calf, and at the hour of the destruction of Jerusalem."

The Baal Shem bade his disciples bare their foreheads, and on every forehead, Sammael saw the sign of the image in which God creates man. He did what was asked of him.

But before leaving, he said, "Sons of the living God, permit
me to stay here a little longer and look at your foreheads."[17]

"In this day and age, when there are no prophets," Rabbi
Bunam once said to his disciples, "how can we tell when a
sin we have committed has been pardoned?"

His disciples gave various answers, but none of them
pleased the rabbi. "We can tell," he said, "by the fact that
we no longer commit that sin."[18]

What I am trying to suggest is that it was not the ideas as such
in the books I was reading that caused me to sense the greatness
of the Judaic religion. It was that in these stories I eventually discovered something about the mind that I had not seen: namely,
that the mind, the intellect, is not simply the logical, analytic, or
even intuitive organ located in the head. The real mind, the real
instrument of understanding, is a blending of at least two fundamental sources of perception—the intellect and the heart; the
intellect and genuine feeling. And I was discovering that genuine feeling is not the same thing as emotional reaction. This to
me was a revolutionary discovery.

It was revolutionary in that the ideal of objectivity, so prized
in modern science and academic study, had degenerated—
profoundly. In the process of trying to free the mind from personal emotions that inevitably bias observation and thought, the
modern ideal of objectivity had unknowingly distanced itself

from a deep, inherent and essential instrument of understanding—what I am calling "genuine feeling."

In this I would cite the words of D. T. Suzuki which over the years have helped me very much. The human mind, he said, has this property, that it asks fundamental questions which the mind alone cannot answer.

A New Judaism and a New Christianity

Was I now ready for Christianity? I had no choice but to try again. The 1965–66 academic year was just beginning and I had already ordered the textbooks for my History of Western Religious Thought course. I was not surprised that the books dealing with Judaism, including, of course, portions of the Old Testament, now had acquired new meaning for me, and I proceeded with a greatly awakened energy to weave my lectures and class discussions around them.

But the Christian texts were another matter. There was, first of all, the New Testament itself. I had been assigning students the Gospel of Matthew, the Gospel of John (especially the opening section dealing with the idea of the Word, or *Logos*—this enabled me to emphasize the philosophical issues related to the ancient Greek meaning of *Logos*)—and also Saint Paul's letters to the Romans and the Corinthians. Far more than with the Old Testament, each time I taught about the New Testament I found it necessary to discuss with the class the whole question of what is scripture. What is a sacred text? How to read it? What makes it "sacred"?

Now, of course, forty or so years later, I am bursting with thoughts, feelings and experiencings that relate to these questions. And this has been so for many, many years, as I will soon explain. But at that time in my life I had very little to bring to that question except a haunting, nearly subconscious sense that I had no right to approach sacred writings merely academically as an object among objects. I had no right to squeeze abstractions, including philosophical conceptualizations, out of them— or, what came to the same thing, to fit them into such abstractions and conventional philosophical problems. I didn't put it to myself in this way exactly, but what I subconsciously felt was that sacred writings were themselves a *Thou*, just as Buber had said about the human being who is my neighbor, or about a tree or, most fundamentally, about God.

It was my new understanding of the Jewish tradition that caused me to see my sense of awkwardness toward the New Testament in these terms—and, of course, my awkwardness toward the figure of Jesus. If the Judaic God was an eternal *Thou*, how much more, perhaps, was the being who, as it was believed, was—as Kierkegaard would have said—the eternal in the form of a human being.

What I didn't yet realize in any but a superficial sense was the obvious corollary of this teaching about *I and Thou*: namely, that in order to open to the *Thou*, I myself, the other half of the relationship, would have to be truly and genuinely **I.** *I would have to be I!* I did not yet realize what this meant. Possibly, in the back of my brain, or somewhere down my spine, Dr. Suzuki was raising the left half of his mouth in his compassionate, semi-merciless Zen smile.

I pondered and pondered, holding the New Testament in my hands, reading in and out of it, picking it up and putting it down. Why did I not feel this awkwardness, this anxious uncertainty about the Old Testament? Why was I unafraid—even eager—to plunge into it with my students? Was the Old Testament not also a sacred book? Of course it was. Did I also feel nervous about "academicizing" it? Not at all, not in the slightest! In fact, it was just because I now sensed the sacredness of the Old Testament that I felt free to bring my love of philosophical ideas into it and to raise every sort of philosophical question in its light. I felt free, absolutely, to bring thought, criticism, doubt, conviction, admiration, reverence, humor—everything my mind was made of—to this sacred book of the religion of my childhood. And that was part of the answer here—it was the book of *my* childhood, *my* people. In that book, now charged with high, exalted mystery and awesome moral demand and bewildering contradictions and charged with all the colors of human life—love, hate, betrayal, vengeance, sex, death, sacrifice . . . in that book were the very roots of my life. I could do as I wished with it; I could do anything except dismiss it—just as, so I then recalled, a Jew can say or think anything about God; he can fight with Him, accuse Him—but he cannot ignore Him. He cannot cease to be a Jew by any action of the energy of his mind. And so my mind was now the mind of a Jew! I would not go to the synagogue or the rabbis; I would not observe the rites and festivals (except, of course, the feeling that rose up from the ground and came down from the sky on Yom Kippur). No, I would not be a "practicing" Jew; but my mind was now suffused with the freedom and even the obligation to think and think well about this God of my fathers and grandfathers. . . .

One needs here to take note of one important aspect of the question of belief in God. Those who deny God (and even as an atheist I never denied the God of my father), those who disprove His existence, who persuade others to deny God—do they have any idea what they are really taking away from people? Do they offer anything to take its place?—anything, that is, that carries with it the flesh and blood of the heart of childhood with all its essence-knowing, its essence-participation in human-ness, its ancient, timeless seeds of love, hope, care: that in childhood which is blended with wind, water, earth and fire? With the sacred physicality of the human body, the tenderness and thunder of animal life and the sweet immensity and power of the green plant?

In any case, picking up and putting down the New Testament, I caught a clear glimpse of my situation. Having felt the sacredness of the Old Testament along with its roots in my own personal history, I was revisited in a much deeper way by my former fear of the New Testament. The last three years, under the demand to teach this course, I had succeeded, on the surface of myself, in regarding both the Old Testament and the New Testament as simply and equally legitimate objects of academic study. But now, suddenly, to teach about the New Testament felt to me like entering an alien country, full of danger. I felt that here there were not just different, and perhaps alien, ideas—but forces, powers, alien energies that I might not be able to deal with or understand, and which might well harm me.

In short, I felt like a spy.

I was taken by the same anxiety, though to a lesser degree, with the other texts that I would be assigning to my students: *Primitive Christianity*, by the renowned twentieth-century Protestant theologian Rudolph Bultmann,[19] and an anthology of writings titled *The Early Christian Fathers*,[20] made up of documents from before the Council of Nicaea in A.D. 325, a period of several hundred years during which, as is now generally understood by the Church, Christianity was explaining and defending its beliefs to the world. And also, important to add, before it began adopting a uniform formulation of dogma. The texts of these early Fathers, however expurgated they may have been, still contain traces of views and insights sometimes startlingly and intriguingly different from what one nowadays generally considers established Christian belief.

I had chosen these texts because each in its way had shown me that Christianity was a matter of thought and not only a matter of what was conventionally understood as faith. Like many,

many other "educated" people, I had come to understand faith as little more than passionate belief lacking all rational or empirical justification. It did not trouble me that throughout the entire world and throughout all of human history millions of people—including almost all of the noblest and wisest men and women—lived by something they called faith. And it did not trouble me especially that Christians considered that having faith—mere unsupported belief—in the divinity of Jesus Christ was enough all by itself to "save" them. I simply accepted all this about faith as only one more sign—a huge sign—of the gullibility and irrationality of most of humanity. Following Sigmund Freud, I felt an occasional pang of condescending compassion for all of humanity that for thousands of years had tried to make sense of life and the world without the benefit of modern science.

Yet, at the same time, I did not and could not accept that the universe was as empty of purpose and consciousness as the universe that science described.

With my new opening to Jewish mysticism, I could and did accept the existence of God, the God that the mystics spoke of, the God portrayed by truly extraordinary ideas about man and the universe, and incarnated in the existence of the remarkable Zen-like rabbis and spiritual masters of Jewish history.

So, now, looking back in time as though through the reverse end of a telescope, I see a plurality of small Jerry Needlemans: one of them totally ignoring or even contemptuous of religious faith, especially the Christian variety; a second Jerry loving what science shows us of the world and nature; a third Jerry refusing to accept the dominant scientific worldview that denies the presence of consciousness and meaning in the universal world; a fourth Jerry, newly minted, who bowed with reverence and wonder in front of the grandeur of the Jewish mystical tradition; and a fifth Jerry who could accept this reverence and wonder only by thinking of the mystical vision as the product of the great imaginative powers of man, not as representing objective truth. As myth, not as fact. Myth in the rather negative sense of the word, as fiction.

I had not yet come to the understanding that genuine myth is one of the principal, absolutely impeccable methods of communicating objective truths to the mind and heart of humanity.

I had not yet come to realize that in perhaps both the positive and negative senses of the word "myth," our present culture was immersed in what can only be called *the myth of the fact.*

In any case, these several Jerrys with their several unrelated attitudes and views about religious faith and truth managed to exist without any common language or communal confrontation within the same brain and body as I rolled up my sleeves and started reading once again, with new, extremely cautious intensity, the textbooks I had assigned to the class—namely, Bultmann's *Primitive Christianity* and the anthology *The Early Christian Fathers.*

I must now mention, however, that there was one other text relating to Christianity that I had placed on the syllabus for the course. But I did not list it as required reading. I listed it only as "recommended." "Recommended" books, books that are not required, but only suggested—books that will not appear on the final exam—are rarely read by students, overburdened as they are with all the other course materials they must master in all their classes. I put it on the syllabus simply because it had been an influential book for me when I had first encountered it. So much so that it was almost as though there was yet another Jerry, a sixth one, who lived somewhere within the covers of this book, but who really had no idea why it was so important. It was almost as though—again more or less subconsciously—this book contained some kind of key that might be able to connect together all the other Jerrys.

That book was *The Gnostic Religion*,[21] by the woefully under-appreciated twentieth-century scholar and philosopher Hans Jonas. Little did I know that in a way I could never have foreseen, this book would lead me to the beginning of an entirely new cycle of my life and to the growth of an entirely new understanding of God.

I will explain this a little later.

But now, however, here I am: Three days a week I am lecturing passionately about the Old Testament, especially the story of Moses and the flight from Egypt; and also submerging myself and my students in the Book of the Prophet Isaiah, while at the same time consulting the koan-like commentaries in the mystical *Zohar* and the stunning glimpses of truth in the tales of the Hasidim. In the evenings, however, I am up late anxiously studying the Gospels, the powerful (but what did they mean?) letters of Saint Paul, and—what was especially decisive—I was poring over great stretches of philosophically sophisticated Christian theology, all the while trying feverishly to acquaint myself with fragments of writings from the early Christian Fathers, writings that I had never imagined, in my wildest fantasies, I would ever read, let alone take seriously.

The irony of it is that when I am reading Christian sources my mind is tightly gripped by the thought contained in the texts of Bultmann and the early "ante-Nicene" Fathers such as Irenaeus, Origen, and Tertullian. And when I am teaching about Judaism, my heart sings and my brain sparkles with the solemn, ecstatic grandeur of meanings hidden under the surface of the Judaic narrative, the Judaic sacredness, the feeling for the real Judaic God that, obviously unbeknownst to me, was inserted into me through my parents and grandparents—inserted somewhere into my psyche, where it took up protected residence like a fugitive waiting in hiding for a chance to return home. The irony is that one of the main ideas I was reading in the Christian texts was that Christianity was totally superior to Judaism—in every way! And not just superior, but that Christianity, especially through Saint Paul, had actually—in the words of the Church historian Adolf von Harnack—freed mankind from what Harnack called "the fetters of Judaism."

Here is an example of how my mind now became so unexpectedly engaged.

The basic idea I was encountering was that Judaism with all

its laws and commandments, all its rituals and rules, with its main concept of God as Creator and Judge, had been valid and adequate only for a certain people and for a certain period of history. But now, with God's incarnation in the person of Jesus Christ, and especially through His crucifixion and resurrection, Christianity had utterly superseded Judaism and offered salvation to all of mankind, not just the people of Israel. The religion of the Hebrew people had, thus, prepared the world for the true religion brought by Jesus Christ, Son of God. Now that this true religion existed on earth, Judaism was at best irrelevant!

During the past three years I had simply brushed past this idea with only a vague sense of distaste. Fine, I said to myself, if that's what Christians want to believe, let them! The Buddhists have their beliefs; the Hindus theirs; the Jews theirs. My job is only to clarify the ideas behind these beliefs and help the students think about their philosophical significance—in this case, perhaps, the Christian idea of the incarnation of God, which, in certain of its aspects, is not unlike the Hindu doctrine of the avatar and the Mahayana Buddhist idea of the incarnation of the cosmic Buddha. Fine. Fine and good.

But now it was not so fine. Yet another Jerry had now appeared who was quite strongly taken by the way this idea was expressed in the writings of Bultmann and in the writings of yet another and even more powerful Protestant theologian, Karl Barth. In fact, I was overjoyed to find that I did not want to simply brush by these ideas that were suddenly touching me almost as strongly as the ideas of the Zen Buddhists and the Jewish mystics. I was overjoyed to find that I could open to Christianity because I now sensed real philosophical thought within it and about it. I had never imagined such a thing, even through the whole process of being educated at some of the finest universities in the world. Throughout the whole of my education Christianity remained something more or less devoid of serious intellectual content. The very notion of theology—thought in the service of faith—was unacceptable to me: How could real thought ever be a servant to blind belief?

But here it was—real thought. It touched my philosophical heart. I could "run with" Christianity now. This appearance of serious thought within the bosom of established Christianity was more important to me (whichever "me" had appeared) than the question of whether the ideas in the writings of Bultmann and Barth and the early Fathers of the Church were true—not only about the world but about their own religion. I could almost say I didn't really care whether or not what they said about Christianity was true or false. What mattered was that it was *interesting!* (I feel pangs of remorse even confessing this now, so many years later, when the question of "interesting" has long since taken a backseat to the question of truth, truth which is another name for the Good).

In any case, here is why this Christian idea about how it differed from Judaism became so interesting to me:

Early on in his book, Bultmann states that by the time of Jesus, the spiritual force of the Judaic idea of God was weakened in the sense that the individual human being was more and more cut off from direct, immediate openness to God. The Judaic God made demands upon man from on high, but He had become less and less accessible as an immediate response to human need. He was no longer, in Bultmann's phrase, the God of the present moment, but only the God of the past and the remote future—and both His cosmic transcendence and the "absurd" legalism of the Pharisaic rules and regulations were such that what was required of man was an impossible act of will in order to *merit* or *earn* His help.

"Thus," says Bultmann,

> ... *repentance itself became a good* work *[that is, requiring something that man must* do *or accomplish] which secured merit and grace in the sight of God. In the end the whole range of man's relation with God came to be thought of in terms of merit, including faith itself. . . . Thus . . . the concept of meritorious faith began to take shape.*[22]

In the proclamation of Jesus, however,

> *[Man] . . . cannot claim anything from God on the ground of personal achievement [and behavior]. . . . God does not claim man only in so far as his behavior is covered [approved] by formulated precepts, as though outside that area [that is, inwardly, apart from external behavior], man were free. [God] forbids not only [the actions of]*

murder, adultery and perjury, but even anger . . . lust and
untruthfulness. His demand embraces not only external
behavior (which the Law can take cognizance of), but
inner motive. God is concerned not only with what man
does, but with the spirit in which he does it.[23]

In such words as these, and all that precedes and follows them in
his book, Bultmann is trying in every way to say something which
can sound as new and radical as, so he believes, the message of
Jesus must have sounded to those to whom he preached it.

I only dimly began to grasp it. For Bultmann (and, in his view,
for Christianity) it is not just man's outer behavior that is at
issue, it is also his inner world—his thoughts, his feelings, his
imagination. "God claims the whole man."

I was a professional philosopher. I was very familiar with the
whole question in the field of ethics of inner motivation and
outer action—Is ethical life to be judged only by deeds, or is it
the motivation that matters most? Yes, I knew about that issue,
that debate.

And no doubt so did Bultmann. Then why was he trying
to make it sound so revolutionary, so new, so astonishing? He
was not naïve. Nor, of course, was Jesus. What was it here that
was supposed to be amazing, astonishing, earthshaking? Because earthshaking it must have been—for someone, say, like
Kierkegaard—and—yes, even for Augustine, the dreaded Saint
Augustine—and even for most of the greatest minds of the last

two thousand years in the West. Why was it supposed to be so radical to speak of motivation as the determining factor of the meaning of human life? And what was so new about the notion that man, as Bultmann put it, "has no freedom over against God. God claims him [man] as a whole. Therefore he [man] cannot claim anything from God . . ."[24]?

I knew, I knew for certain, there was something new here, yet the words and the seeming concepts were so familiar and ordinary—motivation, behavior, merit, judgment. But no, there was something different here. It was the whole question of man's inner life. Man, the individual, I, a human being, had to become different inside myself. But—and I sensed the newness—*I (man) had no control over that!* It was not only that I must not kill, I must not *intend* or *wish* to kill (that was perfectly understandable in any law court)—no, it was that I must not even feel anger and yet—here was newness squared—even that I cannot do; even that I cannot control—*and nothing that I or any human agency could do would give me that power to not feel anger!* And yet, at the same time, I must not feel anger—it is my duty, the demand placed upon me. The demand that comes from God—speaking through Jesus Christ. I cannot do it—yet I *must* do it! I cannot not feel anger, or not crave that woman, or not judge that man; I cannot choose my emotions—yet I must actually do it; I must actually, inwardly forgive at will, intentionally free myself from egoistic impulse of all kinds! That is what man is—that is to say, that is the law under which a human being stands! And under which he is immersed in failure—the word for which is *sin*. The hated word. The deadly word. And yet . . . and yet . . . now becoming so very interesting.

A New Psychology and a New Humanity

It was the same with love. Jesus was commanding man to love God and to love his neighbor and to love all men. How could such love, or any kind of love, be commanded? I am commanded to love my neighbor, to love God. But, in fact, I cannot *do* that—I do not have that power over my deep inner emotional life—*and no human power or human agency could change me, could change a man or woman in that regard!*

I began to sense—so vaguely, in such a slippery, elusive way that it both infuriated and entranced me—that there was something about the inner life, what we call psychology in the modern world, that was being spoken of—and this something was so new, so strange, so difficult to grasp. This was not Freud, this was not Jung, this was not behaviorism. This went deeper, far, far deeper—

But wait! Wasn't this Judaism as well? Wasn't this the heart of Judaism? Or was all of Judaism concerned only with outer behavior after all—just as Bultmann claimed? What about my mystics—weren't they . . . what?

This Jerry, staying up late studying the Christian teachings, could not direct his, my, attention, toward that question (which later opened up in my mind like ten thousand flowers bursting open all at once). This nighttime Christian-Jerry was buffering off the Jewish profundity and being persuaded by this Christian theology, because the Christian theology was awakening in him (in me) a new idea, a new question, so interesting that it engulfed me like fire.

I tore into the book of Karl Barth. Look what he was saying!

In his towering commentary on Paul's Epistle to the Romans, Barth offers a stunning statement of the Christian vision of the inner human condition. The passage in question is Saint Paul's mysterious outcry that continues to echo over the centuries and throughout the nations of the Christian world. In the few years that I had been teaching this material these passages stopped me again and again almost more than any other portion of Christian writings. What did they mean? How could anybody live by them? Were they as perverse as they sounded? I was no stranger to Christian perversity—I had loved Nietzsche's critique of the life-denying Christian teaching. And I had long loved Kierkegaard's flaming sword held to the throat of Christendom. But these passages in Saint Paul were not, in my mind, anything like the sacred "offense" of the Christian paradox that Kierkegaard showed the world. They were simply—weren't they?—nonsense!

But for some reason, the way Barth wrote of them, they started fading, melting, dissolving into a single powerful idea that summoned from me everything my philosophical passion could bring to it.

Here are the passages from Romans. The word "law," in the beginning parts, refers to the Judaic law—the Torah, the Commandments:

> But now we are delivered from the law, that being dead wherein we were held; that we should serve in newness of spirit, and not in the oldness of the letter.
>
> What shall we say then? Is the law sin? God forbid Nay, I had not known sin, but by the law; for I had not known lust, except the law had said, Thou shalt not covet.
>
> But sin, taking occasion by the commandment, wrought in me all manner of concupiscence. For without the law, sin was dead.
>
> For I was alive without the law once; but when the commandment came, sin revived, and I died.
>
> And the commandment, which was ordained to life, I found to be unto death.
>
> For sin, taking occasion by the commandment, deceived me, and by it slew me.
>
> Wherefore the law is holy, and the commandment holy, and just, and good.
>
> Was then that which is good made death unto me? God forbid. But sin, that it might appear sin, working death in me by that which is good; that sin by the commandment might become exceeding sinful.

For we know that the law is spiritual: but I am carnal, sold under sin.

For that which I do I allow not; for what I would, that I do not; but what I hate, that do I.

If then I do that which I would not, I consent unto the law that it is good.

Now then it is no more I that do it, but sin that dwelleth in me.

For I know that in me (that is, in my flesh,) dwelleth no good thing; for to will is present with me; but how to perform that which is good I find not.

For the good that I would I do not; but the evil which I would not, that I do.

Now if I do that I would not, it is no more I that do it, but sin that dwelleth in me.

I find then a law, that, when I would do good, evil is present with me.

For I delight in the law of God after the inward man:

But I see another law in my members, warring against the law of my mind, and bringing me into captivity to the law of sin which is in my members.

O wretched man that I am! Who shall deliver me from the body of this death?

I thank God through Jesus Christ our Lord. . . .

For the law of the Spirit of life in Christ Jesus hath made me free from the law of sin and death. . . .[25]

The law? The law was a demand from above, from God. The demand, as in the prophet Micah, for man "to do justly, and to love mercy, and to walk humbly with thy God." The demand to care for my neighbor and for the stranger; the demand, in the words of all the prophets and all the great teachers of the tradition, not only the teacher Jesus, to be inwardly all that a human being is meant to be as a "son of God." Not only outwardly to do what is good and just, but inwardly to love truth and mercy and duty. Judaism was not only the command to behave in a certain way; it was the demand to be, within oneself, mind and soul, in a certain state of loving obedience to the Good. As in the words of the prophets, who poured out the exclamation from God: "I detest your rites and festivals": that is, our merely external action, usurping the place of the work of obedience to the inner Spirit of God.

Yes, the law is good and holy. The word of God to the Jewish people, to man on earth, is good and holy. But the prophet/apostle Paul—we learn from the theologians, if we haven't seen it for ourselves, as I had not yet seen it—the teaching of Paul is that the entire history of the word of God and man's relation to that word, to that law, that demand to be fully human—the entire history of the law has produced the result that what has been thunderously revealed is man's seemingly intrinsic incapacity actually to live and be according to the law.

Was it so? Could one understand the entire revelation of the Judaic religion to consist not only of the moral law, the law determining the very purpose of human life itself, but also—

and also fundamentally—was the purpose of the law to show man that as he is, we, I, mankind, is unable to conform itself to the law?

God created man to serve, and in that service to live the joy and meaning of his inner divinity. But the discovery of history is that man is unable to serve and unable to be what he is created to be.

Now, here is a small piece of Barth's commentary. My eyes stared, unblinkingly as it seemed, at the printed page:

But the secret he [man] endeavors to conceal cannot be hidden. The bomb, which he has so carefully decked out with flowers, will sooner or later explode. Religion [Judaism] breaks man into two halves. One half is the spirit of the inward man, which delights in the law of God—Am I to identify myself with this spirit? Am I merely [only] inward? But no one dares to make this claim. The other half is the natural world of my members; a world swayed by a wholly different law, by a quite different vitality and possibility. This latter wars against the law of my mind, and denies what it affirms. This corporeality, this essential second factor, this emergent opposition to my soul, is manifestly the supreme law and the supreme human possibility; and here undoubtedly is the sin by which I am imprisoned. Am I to be identified with this sin-laden nature?—Who dares to claim this? The contrast may be defined as inwardness and outwardness, idealism and materialism, that side and this side.[26]

At this Barth puts down his pen and looks up into the eyes of his reader *and at himself*:

> *But to which dost thou belong? Who art thou? Art thou 'Spirit' or 'Nature'? Thou canst not deny 'Spirit', and hold thee only to 'Nature'; for as a religious man, thou hast knowledge of God, and thy most particular perception is that 'Nature' desires to be altogether 'Spirit' [that is, 'Nature' yearns to receive the energies of God]. Neither canst thou deny 'Nature', and hold thee only to 'Spirit'; for, as a religious man, thou hast knowledge of God, and thou knowest only too well that 'Spirit' desires to be altogether 'Nature' [that is, the energies of God yearn to incarnate in 'Nature'].*[27]

And now Barth asks the decisive question, the "One Question" of all human life in relation to one's own individual existence and, as we shall see, in relation to the whole meaning of human life on Earth. We are dealing with two fundamental human and cosmic forces in man and in the universal world: the movement of the descent of the Spirit into the manifest material world (creation, incarnation), and the movement of ascent and return (spiritualization) to the Source that is Spirit, Being itself. And it

is man who is destined to stand in the middle as a bridge between these two intrinsically opposing forces—in Christian language, *on the Cross*:

"Am I then both together?" Barth asks "Well," he answers, "try":

> *Art thou 'Spirit-Nature' or 'Nature-Spirit' . . .? Once*
> *attempt any such arrogant anticipation [that is, once a*
> *man or woman attempts by his or her own power to make*
> *this unification of opposites happen within oneself; once an*
> *individual tries to do what the law has shown us we cannot*
> *do by our own all-too-human effort], then thou wilt soon*
> *perceive that the desired union cannot be maneuvred*
> *merely by ranging the two alongside one another, or by*
> *amalgamating them, or by conglomerating them.*[28]

That is to say: the law has shown us—and universal human experience has shown us—that we are incapable of acting in our
lives according to the good that has been revealed to us.

Barth continues:

> *The more thou dost madly endeavor to synthesize things*
> *which are directly opposed to one another, the more surely*
> *do they break apart and become manifestly antithetic.*
> *And thou thyself art harried hither and thither, from one*
> *to the other. At one moment one has excluded the other—*

and yet not finally or mortally; for when the banished one
seems weakest, there always remains a way for it to return
in the fullness of its power.[29]

Is the situation hopeless? Is there absolutely nothing we can do
to become what we are created to be?

There is nothing we can do.

And yet . . .

Yet there is something that *can be done*—one thing only.
But it is not done by me, by human efforts. It is something
that comes from above, from God—all the way down to humanity in our utter incapacity that inhabits our divine possibility and
obligation.

And here I am standing in front of my class. I have joyously
summed up (that is in my own understanding) what I have
seen to be the essence of Judaism. The students are full of energy and anticipation—

"Judaism," I say, "is the religion of responsibility, the religion
of the *covenant*."

I had already explained to the class the idea of the covenant,
the sacred mutuality between God and Man, wherein God
comes down toward Man—and Man, in holy response, reaches
up toward God.

And here, today, I boldly draw a thick white chalk line on the blackboard, from the very top of the blackboard down, stopping the line halfway. There, at the vertical midpoint, I energetically, in two thick, white strokes, mark the point of an arrow facing down.

Immediately, I start another line, equally thick and strong, starting from the bottom of the blackboard and ending at the very point of the downward line. Here I mark the end of another arrow, marking a movement from the bottom toward the top.

The two arrows meet and touch in the middle.

"This is Judaism," I say. "God comes halfway down, and Man ascends in response halfway up. God reveals the Law, the Torah; Man lives in obedience. The result is . . ."

And here, I suddenly see something. I erase the two arrows. Instead of two strong lines, one moving down and other up, I draw an inverted triangle at the top, symbolizing the same thing as the arrow coming down. And I draw another triangle pointed up at the bottom of the blackboard. And then I draw successive triangles vertically placed under and above the first two triangles representing the movement down from God to Man and also the corresponding movement up from Man to God.

And now the two triangles meet in the middle of the blackboard. And suddenly, like magic, they continue their movement and interpenetrate.

And the class is now looking at the ancient symbol: the six-pointed star! The Star of David.

Shamelessly, without thinking twice about it, I say:

"And here is the central symbol of the central meaning of the Judaic religion: Man and God interpenetrating!"

The shock to the class is considerable. But the shock to me is also considerable. I have made this up. "I have never seen this symbol explained in just this way," I say to the class. "But, take it as a representation of the great Judaic idea of the Covenant between Man and God. God says to Man: I will give you the laws of life; obey my Law, and I promise you in return nothing less than Life.

"Interesting, isn't it?" I say, almost to myself. I have further words to say about this. But I do not say them—words about the meaning of the word "Life" in this context. All I manage to say is that this word does not necessarily mean length of time in years, but something else. I do not want to go into that at that moment. In fact, all I really know is words about the meaning of the ancient word "Life." But it doesn't matter. I have discovered in the moment a meaning, an idea—was it the correct meaning? That was not important to me then and there. My mind was alive and engaged. I could have easily given a serious philosophical explanation of these ideas, bringing in many great thoughts from the philosophers and many important conceptual distinctions in the realm of ethics and metaphysics. . . .

But already I am—in one sudden stroke—dramatically erasing the whole diagram—the triangles, the six-pointed star!

The students are taken aback. What is Professor Needleman up to?

"And here," I announce, "here is Christianity."

Holding the chalk lengthwise against the top of the blackboard, I make a three-inch-wide solid white line from the top of the blackboard all the way down to the very bottom, where I mark in another vivid white arrowhead, the point of which touches the lower metal frame of the blackboard.

"Here is Christianity. Here is the message of Paul. *The Law has shown that Man is incapable of obeying the Law.* And so God comes all the way down to Man! Jesus Christ is God coming all the way to me. Man is not required to do anything; he has shown that he is incapable. And so the Father sends the Son all the way into the flesh of Man. This is the meaning of the word *grace*— the gift from Above, the *unearned* gift. All that Man has to do is to *receive, accept* that gift. That is the meaning of the Christian idea of faith—an act of pure receiving of the gift. The Greek word is *pistis.* Quite different in meaning from the Hebrew word, *emunah,* meaning "trust," a word appropriate to a covenant between two parties. The Christian faith begins by recognizing that the gift has already been given without Man performing any actions (of which he is incapable)."

The bell rings, ending the class. I am happy. My mind is alive. I am buoyed up by the irresistible anticipation of thinking as deeply as I can about both Judaism and Christianity. In that sense, I have accepted Christianity—not that I will become a Christian. That is not at all important. No, what is important is that my mind is fully engaged; I am ready to think, to question, to see connections, to help my students, to understand something central about this mysterious, hitherto alien and dangerous dominant religion of the Western world, the religion that haunted my childhood like an occupying enemy force.

I am happy.

But . . . but . . . what is this hollow feeling right under the surface of my happiness?

CHAPTER FIVE

Beyond the Hollow Mind: The Idea of God

What is God?

I had no suspicion that my personal discovery of the intellectual content of Judaism and Christianity was mirroring, in its own small way, an immense struggle that shaped the heart of our whole Western civilization two thousand and more years ago. I had no suspicion that the word "God," which we all take for granted, was, as an idea, actually the work of many gifted minds searching, pondering, plunging themselves into the depths of meditation and contemplation while submitting to the stringent demands of philosophical dialogue, argument and objective logical reflection. We use the word "God" and rarely ask ourselves what is really meant by that word. We assume we understand the meaning of the word simply because we know how to use it in conventional contexts and grammatically correct sentences. But many of us have little conception of all that the idea contains and all the questions and answers that are part of it. And above all, many of us—at least it was so for me—are not aware of the inner experience that validates the idea, that shows the way toward impartial verification of the existence of that which we can justifiably and with good conscience call *God*.

The early centuries of the Christian religion, and therefore of what we call our "Christian era," are permeated, defined, by the question of how to think about God—and not only *how* to think about God, but, and this is of paramount importance, *whether* to think about God. The writings of the "early Christian Fathers" may be understood as one vast effort to find the place of philosophy in the expression and transmission of the Christian religion. That is: to find the place of ancient Greek thought, especially the philosophy of Plato, in the articulation of the teachings of the Church. And that is further to say, more simply and more fundamentally, to find the place of the intellect itself, of the mind itself, in the search for God, in the individual lived life, in the struggle for a meaningful, fulfilling, fully human life—in the need and struggle to live rightly amid all the forces of everyday human existence, the existence made up of love, desire, fear, man and woman, children, wealth and neediness, the body and its pleasures and pains, and—perhaps above all—the confrontation with one's own inevitable death and the death of those one loves—in short, human life in all its impermanence, all its fullness and emptiness. What *is* the role of the mind in front of all this concrete reality of hope and despair, war, violence, disillusionment, sadness, grief, pleasure that decays into the slavery of craving; certainties that decay into rigid prejudices; love that turns to bitterness and hatred; loyalties that are devastated by betrayals; the human life of lies and half-truths, of false self-confidence? Can the mind alone guide a man or woman through all this and a thousand other such elements that make up what we call our human life—that is, the *world?* The world we live in and that lives in us—that *is* us. The world that the Apostle Paul and others called *the flesh.*

The idea of God, apparently so simple an idea, was brought to humanity—who knows by whom?—in order to guide human beings through the vast tunnels and labyrinths of individual and communal human life. It was the work of these early Christian Fathers, through the instrument of philosophy, to connect the idea of God to all these thousand aspects of human life—the meaning of death, the principles of virtuous living, the duties and obligations to family, friends, and enemies, the relationship to nature, to wealth, to hunger, to pleasure, to the wish to love and be loved. Through this program of establishing the relationship between the idea of God and all the facets of human life, the idea itself of God was broadened, deepened and refined.

Of course, the most fundamental element of the Christian life remained the pure act of faith, the direct feeling and opening to the sacred events and the divinity of Christ as the Son of God. But now faith was no longer partitioned off from the full reach of human concerns. As had been the case in Judaism, the idea of God now began to embrace and influence the whole rough and tumble of life in all its raw and refined details. The idea of God began to define the very perception of reality, the nature of knowledge, the meaning of art and craft, the meaning of citizenship and political life, the purpose of education, etc., etc.

The idea of God became such as to introduce the possibility that there was nothing in human life at all that could be understood without ultimate and fundamental reference to this higher reality called God. The question began to be introduced into developing Western civilization that human life itself, human nature itself was meaningless and futile without an *obedient reference* to God—if not through direct experience of God, then through the authority of principles, doctrines and rituals formulated and laid down ultimately by those who had indeed been privileged to speak from direct experience. The ultimate power and mission of the Church over the centuries is and was rooted in this vision of the all-inclusive *authority*, in all things and all aspects of life, of the power and the love of God.

Because of this, the question arises for us, as it must also have arisen in antiquity, of what that "obedient reference" actually means. It could mean everything from a fanatical adherence to a subjective, self-serving appropriation of the idea of God, turning it into a mad tool of the individual or collective ego—or it could mean something extraordinarily fine and rare, and subtle, defining the meaning of human existence through the work of establishing in oneself an opening to an unknown higher influence which the whole complex of the human body and all of human functioning was designed to serve. Between these two extremes—the idea of God as an instrument of madness and the idea of God as a symbol of inner sanctity and true being— between these two extremes the idea of God has swung wildly back and forth through the centuries and within almost every era of our history. Between these two extremes, as we may reasonably speculate, there exists a profusion of shades and degrees. So much so that for a long time the idea of God, the word itself, has taken on as many connotations and denotations as there are types and gradations of the human psyche. To the point that the word itself, the notion itself of God, means almost anything one wants it to mean. To the point that we can say, without much exaggeration, that the word itself has become meaningless—that is, that it can mean anything to anyone. And therefore, in order to think about God, we must think about many other things and ideas as well—ultimately, we must think about *everything*, about the laws and principles that govern everything! We must think about the sky and the oceans and the earth, the world of nature, human history, art, the human body, the meanings of beauty, social organization, the nature of friendship and love—everything. Such is one of the fundamental meanings of the work of philosophy. And this means, necessarily, that we must learn how to think, about what to think, and what inner demand upon ourselves is necessary in order to think well and fully, like human beings, and not like domestic animals or computers.

And it will turn out that one of the very first steps in learning how to think about God is to realize that the isolated intellect is incapable of going beyond a certain point in the work of thinking about reality. It will turn out that we need much more of the whole human psyche—which includes the function of authentic, non-egoistic feeling—to think about God. The isolated intellect, devoid of contact with the power of real, non-egoistic feeling, may ultimately be incapable of thinking past the most elementary stages in this task. Without much exaggeration, we can even say that the isolated mind, the head unconnected to the power of non-egoistic feeling, and dependent only upon primitive impressions brought by the external senses, the mechanical rules of logical forms, and the automatic associations of words and images—we may say that this mind is, intrinsically, an atheist.

This is the hollow mind.

About the inescapable role of the human body in the attainment of knowledge we will speak later.

Another Kind of Knowing

The class assignment was to read numerous excerpts from the writings of second- and third-century Christianity—writings by men whose names are generally unknown to any but theologians, scholars of religion, and historians of late antiquity; names that have rarely been heard even once by many highly educated people in our modern world: names such as Irenaeus, Clement of Alexandria, Tertullian, and that most dynamic mystical rationalist, Origen. In these writings you find the idea of God conjoined with specific and pointed knowledge about the nature of society, the human body, sexuality, ethics, the structure of the cosmos, the meaning of love and death, the emotions. Here you find a vast system of questions and answers about the soul, questions and answers that comprise an extraordinary vision which includes and also transcends what we conventionally call the science of psychology and states of consciousness. All of this and more enters into the idea of God that is being developed and clarified through the heroic attempt to infuse philosophical thought into the Christian idea of God. The heroic attempt to marry the act of faith with the proper work of the mind.

It was during one of my lectures about the early Christian Fathers that I happened to write the word "Gnosticism" on the blackboard. As is now widely known, due in part to the pioneering books of Elaine Pagels, "Gnosticism" is a term applied to a wide variety of religious teachings that flourished in the early centuries of Christianity and competed with the fledgling Church when it was in the early stages of securing its place in the currents of Western civilization. Because of their sometimes startlingly different interpretations of the message and nature of Christ, and because of their emphasis on knowledge rather than faith, and because of their sometimes bewildering and/or apparently offensive ritual customs, these religious teachings were treated as heresies and more or less ferociously hounded out of existence or driven into hiding. Almost all of their Scriptures were destroyed as well as almost all first-hand accounts of their ways of life.

Much of what we know of these teachings is based on accounts by Christian writers intent on refuting their ideas and condemning their practices. So it is safe to say that this source of information may very possibly blind us to whatever in their practice and ideas was not only honorable but even perhaps authentically "esoteric"—that is, representing an understanding available only as a result of precise inner spiritual discipline and often expressed, as has been the case throughout history, in "encoded" symbols and narratives. The purpose of such encoded writing is twofold. While illuminatingly clear to followers engaged in the process of their inner self-struggle, it serves at the same time to protect powerful spiritual ideas from being wrongly and superficially appropriated by the isolated, egoistic intellect and the world at large. In which case, instead of helping people on the way to true devotion and inner freedom, they become a source of self-deception and fanaticism.

The Gnostic Religion

Perhaps the main aspect of these Gnostic religions is what has been seen as their claim to possess and transmit a special kind of knowledge (the Greek term is *gnosis*) which differs markedly from what the word represents in the modern world. Gnosis is a term meant to designate what we may call "salvational" or, more precisely, *transformational*, knowledge—knowledge the possession of which transforms the intrinsic character or level of being of the individual. Such knowledge is not simply knowledge as it is understood in the modern world, namely a property of the intellect alone, which the individual may then act upon in order to discover new truths or to solve problems or invent instruments and programs designed to produce desired results, such as new technologies. Such knowledge, in the modern, conventional meaning of the word, refers to an object outside of the knowing subject, outside of the knower. Gnosis, on the other hand, transforms the knower as well as that which is known. In gnosis, subject (the knower) and object (that which is known) are one.

It would not be entirely amiss to speak of gnosis as representing a mystical conception of knowledge. Taken in this sense, the word gnosis refers to an aspect of every great spiritual and religious tradition the world has ever known. The use of the word to refer to certain sects and teachings that abounded in the early Christian era should not blind us to the more universal and fundamental meaning of the term.

Historical, theological, and scholarly accounts of Gnosticism in the early Christian era often present us with a bewildering and bizarre picture of wildly fanciful symbolisms, mythologies, religious claims, philosophical incoherence, and even coarse, repellent sectarian practices and exercises. No doubt such a picture is largely due to the fact that most of the accounts we have are by writers intent on discrediting these teachings. On the other hand, it is certainly clear that in the early centuries of our era, the Roman empire in the Mediterranean crescent, from Athens to

Alexandria, Persia, Syria, and Jerusalem, abounded in religions, sects and schools of every stripe and form—perhaps many, if not most, of dubious nature. We need only look at our own contemporary invented mysticisms and vicious fundamentalisms.

Yet then, as now, there surely existed among all these "new religions" and "esoteric" teachings, some—perhaps only a few—which were genuine spiritual teachings emanating from a higher source. In my own mind, as I saw things then, I admitted to myself that I could not really distinguish the authentic from the inauthentic in all these bewildering accounts and surviving fragments of spiritual revelations and philosophical speculation. All I could say was that I certainly did not feel that all these "Gnostic" teachings were false and the Church alone was true. Some of the surviving material in these Gnostic teachings was deeply moving to me—even though much was strange and incomprehensible. I felt only a glimmering understanding that many of the writings and mythologies of the Gnostics were symbolic of processes and forces and situations within the self, expressed as narratives about the universal cosmos. It only vaguely occurred to me that in such narratives—as was much more clearly the case in the Jewish mystical texts that had enthralled me—an account of the human situation and its possible healing and transformation was being offered in cosmic, metaphysical language, symbolically, allegorically.

It only dimly occurred to me that the ancient Greek discovery of the power of rationalistic, scientific thought and language had been necessary to liberate the mind from the superstition and naïve literalism that had become rampant in their culture. And that our own modern scientific language and thought, as it was also embodied in the modern idea of philosophy, had served the same honorable purpose in our culture. But the fact remained that spiritual ideas, ideas meant to move and actually guide men and women toward the work of inner liberation and transformation, were relatively rarely expressed in ancient times in the language of rationalism. Great ideas from authentic spiritual traditions embodying a genuinely higher kind of knowledge were almost always communicated through myth and story and powerful imagery—just in order to allow the teaching to touch the feeling heart, rather than submit to capture and encapsulation by the head, where such knowledge would ultimately serve only to fortify man's illusions about himself and his egoistic impulses toward his neighbor.

I see now that it was this aspect of some of the Gnostic material that was touching me in a way I could not deny, even though I was preconditioned to regard it all with great suspicion and even mockery. Something in me semiconsciously recognized and felt that some of these images and narratives were about *me*. Not long after, I came to realize that it was just this kind of recognition that was at the root of my discovery of the power of the Old Testament and the Kabbalah and, yes, the New Testament and the sacred story of Christ.

Here I can give only a tiny sample of some themes and passages from the Gnostic texts that transcend all easy judgments of "heresy," "superstition" or "irrationalism." To make my point about some of this material, I have chosen a few texts which are relatively free of the mythic/symbolic terminology involving forces, principalities, powers, and evil gods and demons imprisoning man in the world of matter, as well as salvational forces and benign alien gods of love liberating the human soul from the merciless laws of the cosmos and the "vain creator God" of the Bible.

A common theme is that Man is alone and imprisoned in a world that is mortally inimical to his true Self:

> *I am I, the son of the mild ones [i.e., the beings of Light]. Mingled am I, and lamentation I see. Lead me out of the embracement of death.*[30]

> *A vine am I, a lonely one, that stands in the world. I have no sublime planter, no keeper, no mild helper to come and instruct me about every thing.*[31]

Equally pervasive is the notion that human beings are "asleep" in the world. "Men are not just asleep, but 'love' the sleep.". . . However, "even realizing that sleep is the great danger of existence in the world is not enough to keep one awake, but it prompts the prayer":

> *According to what thou, great Life, saidst unto me, would that a voice might come daily to me to awaken me, that I*

*may not stumble. If thou callest unto me, the evil worlds
will not entrap me and I shall not fall prey to the Aeons.*[32]

*What, then, is that which He [the Lord, God, Christ]
desires man to think? This: "I am as the shadows and
phantoms of the Night." When the light of dawn appears,
then this man understands that the Terror which had
seized him was nothing. . . . As long as ignorance
inspired them with terror and confusion, and left them
unstable, torn and divided, there were many illusions
by which they were haunted, and empty fictions, as if they
were sunk in sleep and as if they found themselves a prey
to troubled dreams. Either they are fleeing somewhere, or
are driven ineffectually to pursue others; or they find
themselves involved in brawls, giving blows or receiving
blows; or they are falling from great heights . . . [etc., etc.]:
until the moment when those who are passing through all
these things wake up. Then those who are experiencing all
these confusions, suddenly see nothing. For they are
nothing—namely, phantasmagoria of this kind.*[33]

*If a person has the Gnose [salvational knowledge], he is a
being from on high. If he is called, he hears, replies, and
turns toward Him who calls him, in order to reascend to
Him. And he knows what he is called. Having the Gnose,
he performs the will of Him who called him. He desires*

to do that which pleases Him, and he receives repose
[inner peace]. Each one's name comes to him. He who thus
possesses the Gnose, knows whence he is come and where
he is going.[34]

Certain elements in these Gnostic writings reminded me of the
terminology employed by G. I. Gurdjieff, whose teaching a few
years before had been an intense interest of mine. Gurdjieff, too,
had diagnosed the human condition as a state of waking sleep in
which the whole of man's life is mechanically ruled by the "principalities and powers," or cosmic forces, of a world itself lost
in illusion and meaninglessness. For Gurdjieff, it seemed, as it
was for the Gnostics, the whole aim of human life was to receive
the help offered to man by a higher knowledge in order to struggle against these forces and awaken to the Self within oneself.

And so, without thinking twice about it, I wrote the name
of Gurdjieff on the blackboard. "The teaching of Gurdjieff," I
said to the class, "is a contemporary example of Gnosticism."
Even as I said it, however, I felt the superficiality of that remark.

In any case, at the end of the class, as the students were filing
out the door, one of them came up to me and stood across
my desk looking at me, quietly waiting for the classroom to be
empty. He was tall, thin, slightly stooped, looking a bit older
than he probably was—maybe in his mid twenties—with dark
eyes in a pale narrow face.

When he was absolutely sure no one else was in the room,

he asked me, almost in a whisper, "How do you know about Gurdjieff?"

I stood up, gathering my papers and putting them in my briefcase. I smiled at him and said, taking a little pleasure in being somewhat nonchalant and even a bit dismissive, "Oh, yes, I know about the Gurdjieff ideas and the Work."

This was in the 1960s, several years before the wave of new (to the West) Eastern religious teachings and new spiritually defined communal experiments began taking root in and around San Francisco. At that time, groups studying the Gurdjieff teaching kept very much to themselves and even the name "Gurdjieff" was mostly unknown and, where known, the object, often, of mistrust and misunderstanding due to fantastic rumors about the man and his teaching that were spread during the early years of his work in France in the 1920s. Certainly, his teaching was totally unrecognized and out of place in any respectable academic context, be it philosophy, religious studies, sociology, or psychology. The mention of his name was obviously a distinct shock to the student standing across from me, who let it be known that he was "in the Gurdjieff Work," as it was called.

"Do you know this book?" he asked, handing me a slender volume with a totally black dust jacket. I politely looked at it. All I recognized was the name of Gurdjieff as I hastily shook my head no and started to hand it back to him. "Would you like to borrow it?" he asked, with touchingly modest earnestness. As a kindness to him, I held on to it and placed it in my briefcase.

"Thank you," I said, and thought nothing further of it.

A New Part of the Mind

The book was called *Our Life with Mr. Gurdjieff*,[35] written by the Russian composer Thomas de Hartmann. Glancing through it, I saw that it was a newly published autobiographical narrative of how Gurdjieff led a small group of his first pupils on a dangerous and demanding escape from war-torn Russia at the onset of the Russian Revolution. Journeying by foot over the Caucasus mountains, and then, afterward, dispersing via Constantinople, they were led, finally, to France, where Gurdjieff established his "Institute for the Harmonious Development of Man" in a village outside Paris. I put the book down at the corner of my crowded desk and left it there without opening it again.

I was already quite familiar with what I took to be the main book about the Gurdjieff teaching, *In Search of the Miraculous* by P. D. Ouspensky.[36] It was that book which, some eight years before, in 1957, had drawn me to seek out the Work in New York. It had made an extremely strong impression on me. Although many of the ideas in it struck me as outlandish, many others were startlingly insightful—ideas about the human psyche unlike anything I had ever encountered in the writings of psychologists or in what I had seen in the teachings of the great spiritual traditions of the world, including Zen Buddhism. I was suspicious of what the book said about the need for an "esoteric" school based on knowledge of a "higher level" than anything that could be found in our contemporary world. But while entertaining heavy doubts and suspicions, I was being bombarded on nearly every page by stunning explanations that put in question one after another of my philosophical assumptions and convictions about, so it seemed, nearly everything I believed. The more I read, the more I was both troubled and inwardly moved by the intimation of an invisible and immense coherence of thought behind all that was being said.

But the most remarkable thing about the book was what emerged in it about the figure of Gurdjieff himself. The way I put it to myself was that he spoke *with authority.* I won't attempt here to explain or justify that statement beyond saying that it was a *feeling.* And that feeling itself had a kind of action upon me, a quality of authority that ordinary emotions, even at their most intense, did not have. This sense of inner authority existed within me alongside all of the doubts and questions and convictions I naturally had as a well-educated, well-trained student of philosophy. This feeling of authority did not, so to say, attempt to overpower or refute all my own ideas and acquired convictions. It just existed—shall I say, "radiated"?—calmly inside my mind and in some strange way permitted, and in some sense contained, all my familiar thoughts about God and everything else. It was like discovering not so much new ideas or a new philosophy, but—if I may put it this way—it was like discovering a new part of my mind.

At that time, in 1957, I had attended meetings at the Gurdjieff Foundation in New York for about eight months, coming down once a week by train from New Haven. Eventually I found what I took to be the "work" too difficult—not physically, but emotionally, or perhaps I should say "existentially." This, too, I understood only much later.

In any case, it was shortly after I stopped going to these meetings that I met with the Zen Buddhist scholar D. T. Suzuki. My initial disappointment with that meeting effectively put an end to my hopes of or interest in finding and pursuing a practical spiritual quest. I steered my ship back toward academic philosophy at Yale. At the same time, however, I called forth an old dream of mine and started writing a novel, which I called *The Golden Person*. This phrase, "the golden person," is often used in translating the Sanskrit word *atman*, meaning the higher Self or God within man. The novel was centered around a beautiful, charismatic mystic whom I had known when I was only seventeen years old and who claimed to be able to see all people in terms of what she said was their "level of being." I had briefly fallen under her spell and was shocked to learn several years later that she had committed suicide. The novel was to be about the human futility of seeking to transcend this concrete, earthly life through mystical experience. That is, I continued to try to think about God, but only through the medium of writing imaginative literature that in some way justified my failure to find God.

But now here I was sitting after dinner in my comfortable armchair happily preparing the next day's class dealing with one or another Judaic or Christian text—I forget exactly which. By now I had completely made my peace with religion, both the religion of my childhood and the formerly suspect and threatening Christian religion. I had discovered something of the great ideas about man and the universe lying at the heart of these religions. Ideas that I could respect. And work with. Ideas that told me something of great philosophical importance about humanity and God.

Had I become a "believer"? No. Was I still what I called an "atheist"? No to that also. Then what was I?—some kind of "agnostic"? No, not that either. Because I knew that God was something real in the life of man and in the life of the mind. Only fools denied the intrinsic importance of religion and the idea of God. But—yes, this too—only fools (in my judgment) swallowed it all whole and took it all literally as objectively true.

But again: What was I? Well, I could tell myself (had I had the sincerity to ask this of myself) that I believed in man, in the uniquely human—in the power of the human heart and mind to create and form symbols and meanings. I could tell myself that I loved truth. That it was possible to find personal meaning in the depth of the mind and in the depth of love. As for reality itself, the objectively known world, the world that science presented to us, the fact was, perhaps, that man lived and died within a blind and purposeless universe. But did that really matter?—or, rather, did it matter so much that one had simply to accept it and then forget it, and go on, and in, and deep down to the greatness of this poor doomed metaphysical anomaly called Man, Man the creator of meaning and purpose? That was where "God" lived—deeply and beautifully in my Judaism and my (now) Christianity, in the beautiful enlightenment of the Buddha and Zen, and in the great golden person, Atman, of the Hindu imagination . . . etc.

That was my so-called "worldview." What shall I call it? Spiritual humanism? Spiritual secularism?

God? Objectively, maybe God did not exist—but did that really matter? Truth was more important than "God." Wasn't it? Man would die. I would die. Everything would die. But now, here, I existed and I would become man.

Something like that.

My eyes fell on the book about Gurdjieff on my desk, where I had placed it two weeks before. Every day now in class the student who had loaned it to me would anxiously scan me, looking for signs that I was reading it. Well, why not? I went over to my desk and then settled down in my armchair and started reading.

My first impression of the book was its simplicity and artlessness. The author was obviously not a sophisticated writer, but there was something clean in his words as he spoke of his first meeting with Gurdjieff and of the certainty he and his young wife had felt about Gurdjieff's knowledge and spiritual presence. I effortlessly read further about the small group that gathered around Gurdjieff and about their abrupt preparations for escaping the fast-approaching revolutionary upheaval. I read about the physical difficulties experienced by the young composer and his wife, accustomed as they were to social privilege and luxury, who now were obliged to walk day and night over mountains and through rough forest terrain, their bodies aching and their feet raw and sore. And I read how, in the midst of great difficulty and extreme danger, they placed complete trust in the man they called "Mr. Gurdjieff." Trust not only in his resourcefulness and practical skill, but in the attitude he cultivated in them that enabled them to regard everything they were experiencing first and foremost as material for self-knowledge and what Gurdjieff called "self-remembering."

At the same time, I was unexpectedly touched by what I only now can call the unspoken moral force that passed between Gurdjieff and his companions. This completely new quality of morality was somehow blended with the personal rigor and firmness of Gurdjieff's demands and his apparently phenomenal knowledge of the human psyche, as well as with the sense of great physical danger in a world suddenly falling apart, surrounded by the psychosis of revolution and war that could break murderously upon the small band of travelers at any moment. And there, at the same time, was Gurdjieff's gentleness, as unexpected and deep as were the demands he placed upon his pupils' stamina and personal fiber. All under the dark, soft southern skies full of stars.

I stayed in my chair reading, hours into the night. Never before had a book extracted from me this particular quality of attention. I was in no way "devoured" by it in the way I had been engulfed by the powerful mystical and spiritual books of Judaism and Christianity—or Zen Buddhism, for that matter. I did not continually put the book down and think and ponder and associate about the people and the events. I was quite aware of my surroundings and of myself sitting in the chair—even though the narrative was full of vivid events: near-death experiences, bandits with rifles, warlike Cossacks and Red Russian soldiers. The book was filled as well with the numerous uniquely powerful emotional demands in the embrace of which Gurdjieff would little by little transmit the meaning of his ideas. Even with all this I never forgot that I was sitting there . . . in my chair . . . in the middle of the night. The more I read, the more I sensed my own presence. And the more I sensed a strong, indefinable *goodness* in what I was reading—and, uniquely, in myself.

Several days later, after class, as the students were filing out, I called over the student who had loaned me the book. "Thank you," I said, handing it back to him.

"What did you think of it?" he asked.

I didn't know what to say. I settled for a warm "I found it very interesting." But after he left, as I was still standing alone at my desk, I recognized to my great surprise what the book had meant to me.

It made me quiet.

Part Two

CHAPTER SIX

The Question Within the Question

More than sixty years have passed since that summer night in Philadelphia when I was sitting on stone steps next to my father; when for a few moments millions of stars appeared in the sky and I heard my father say in an unusual voice, "That's God." It was only then, on that summer night, that I silently, quietly, sensed that the question of God is also a question about myself. Who am I? Why do I exist?

More: under that sky, under the question of God I sensed the seed of another question, a question hidden within the question of God and myself, a question that only much later began to ripen and show its authority in my life. Words cannot really convey its authority unless it is being experienced in the moment: Not *why* do I exist? But *do* I exist?

There is a tremendous secret hidden in this apparently absurd question. It will take some time to try to explain it and to explain why the question of God, the question of the existence of God that has tormented philosophers and others for centuries, the question of good and evil—why does God allow evil, why does God allow suffering, the suffering of innocents, etc.—it will take time to explain why throughout an individual's own life and throughout human history itself, the question of God cannot be approached past a certain severe limit without seriously confronting this apparently absurd question. I mean to say that at a certain point in an individual's thought and life, as well as at certain definite moments in the history of cultures, the human mind and heart inevitably—with very few exceptions—come face-to-face with a wall beyond which they cannot go. Whether this wall takes the form of futile or facile attempts to prove or disprove the existence of God, or whether it takes the form of the question of evil and injustice, or whether it takes the form of the riddle of death, or despair or fear or dreamy fantasy, or self-pity or pain and loss, or the stupidity of the mass mind and its addiction to violence—these are all segments of the same wall that at some point inevitably appears when a man or woman tries honorably to think about God.

Within the silence of that question of one's own being, all the other questions of the heart take on calm light, like candles burning in a sacred space. I mean to say that without confronting this hidden question-within-the-question-of-God, this seemingly absurd question, there will never be any possibility of answering the question of God. There will be doubters and believers; there will be good and bad people; there will be bloody war and inconceivable cruelty in the name of God; there will be "weeping and gnashing of teeth"; there will be proofs and denials, some clever, some fantastic; there will be a suffocating planet gasping for air and a suffocating humanity gasping for meaning. And, unknown to us, all this will take its dark strength only in the unlit shadow that is the absence of this hidden question. In that shadow, in the absence of this hidden question, all the unique energies and possibilities of human nature, deprived of their proper light and nourishment, grow into strange and often monstrous forms, all subsumable under one term: barbarism.

In speaking of this question-within-the-question, I am pointing toward a new conception of God desperately needed in our life and our world.

The Future of an Illusion

I think now of all that has passed both in our personal lives and in the life of our world in the past half-century or so. In the years when I was still a young professor of philosophy—just beginning to perceive the immense depths of the religions that I had till then dismissed—at that time the general view of the academic and scientific establishment was that religion was a cultural relic well on its way to being marginalized in the advancing life of modern civilization. Religion, and the idea of God, as Freud had so confidently prophesied, were being replaced by scientific, purely humanistic thought as an arbiter of values and truth.

As for myself, what was happening to me was just the opposite of what Freud had predicted for our culture, although in my case what was involved was not a matter of religious faith, but of concrete experience, as concrete and real in its way as anything science offered. The starting point in my experiential, *empirical* understanding of the idea of God began with the experience I have described at the end of the previous chapter, an experience at that time unique in my adult life—the experience of a truly quiet mind. I soon after came to realize that in this experience of a quiet mind I could have said, without lying or pretense, or mere intellectualizing, "I exist." I could have answered the impossible question that had been put to me by Dr. Suzuki.

It took me many years to see that what I had long ago as a child understood to be God was now moving on its labyrinthine way into my adult life, gradually becoming an active influence in my mind and in my relationship to all that I loved and cared for. But for many years it did not and could not carry the name "God." And the fact that this experience of a quiet mind was not for me in the least associated with anything "religious" was an essential element in the mercy of that labyrinthine path which I had begun to follow and certain aspects of which I will try to describe in these pages. I will try to describe elements of this path not merely because of what it meant to me personally, but because of what it can mean to our suffocating world.

Freud's prophecy and the self-assured "establishment" consensus about the diminishing future of religion in the age of science began coming into question for me with the appearance of "new" Eastern religions in the late 1960s. It was, of course, a time of seething turmoil in America. The much-hated Vietnam War was in full throttle, bringing with it the explosion of long

pent-up moral and spiritual dissatisfaction, especially in the rising generation. The image of America as the hope of the world
was being shaken to its foundations; the static moralism and
legalism enshrouding family, sexuality and institutional authority were being torn away.

I was fortunate to be living in San Francisco, the epicenter of
this "spiritual revolution" as it flamboyantly called itself. But even
with all the gullibility, foolishness and fraudulence surrounding
this "spiritual revolution"—even with all the half-, quarter-, and
zero gurus gathering their spiritually starving young followers—
even within the chemical blood and smoke of psychoactive
drugs—it gradually became clear to me that something of great
importance was trying to break through the cultural armor of our
society.

I say "gradually" because at first I was simply repelled, or
condescendingly amused, by white-robed Hinduized college-
aged men and pretty, young women chanting Sanskrit man-
tras on downtown street corners; I was deeply troubled by the
drug-glazed eyes that met me not only in the Haight-Ashbury
but often in my classroom; I was cynically indifferent to all
the experiments in "spiritual" communal living sprouting in and
around San Francisco; I was secretly jealous and a little frightened in front of the sexual liberty and availability of the women.
And as for the teachers and gurus who were pouring in from
Asia, even though they might have come to America from
within a genuine religious tradition, I somehow could not or
would not take them seriously. Of course, it was not too long

before I discovered that among them were men and women of great character and sincerity, and not a few bearing considerable wisdom and moral power. But at the beginning I painted it all with the same broad brush: one more naïve, desperate belief in religion—what matter that it was Eastern religion in this case?—as the answer to all the problems of life and the world. I made no connection in my mind between this "spiritual revolution" and what I had discovered in Jewish mysticism or in the teachings of Saint Paul or in special elements of Gnosticism or in the writings of the early Christian Fathers. Nor, strangely enough, did I feel in this movement any resonance with my encounter with D. T. Suzuki and Zen Buddhism—even though followers and teachers of Zen Buddhism were very much a part of the "spiritual revolution."

I did not at first see the mind or feel the quiet heart of truth in any of it. I saw only the self-advertised surfaces and felt only the agitation—happy though it sometimes seemed and promising all forms of pleasure along with enlightenment, but in fact also bringing with them anger, greed, exploitation, and uncontrolled fantasy. Along with a mixed but often genuine love of the Earth and resentment toward the self-betrayal of America, I saw thrusts of courage, boldness, tenderness, but also carelessness, ignorance, and paranoia. I saw the yearning for justice, the hatred of prejudice, the total incapacity to make real changes in the larger life of the world, yet the willingness to spill one's own blood if necessary to help the world, the poor, the oppressed, the plundered Earth. I saw naïveté about what makes the world turn: money, cunning, deception, politics . . . insanity.

In short, I at first felt that the whole world, with all its chaos and false promises, was more or less recapitulating itself in this movement, only now with new religious or "spiritual" coloration. And the whole world was the problem, not the solution, even if the solution was now phrased in Eastern religious language and certain forms of pious behavior. Freud was still secure in his place, with only a few clouds in his sky, clouds easily dismissed, were they not?

"You Yourselves Do Not Exist"

Nor did I see or feel much connection in any of this with what I was coming to understand and experience of the Gurdjieff teaching—although it was through the help of that teaching that many years later I became certain of the existence of God. Had not Gurdjieff emphatically distanced his teaching from religion in all its known forms? Had he not spoken, even more forcefully perhaps than Freud and Nietzsche, of the hypocrisy, self-deception and suggestibility that had eaten away almost all that may once have been real and authentic in the religions of our era?

Three years had passed since I had renewed my interest in Gurdjieff. Very soon after returning the book, *Our Life with Mr.*

Gurdjieff, to the student who had pressed it upon me, I was standing in my office at home in front of a wall of books, looking for
my old copy of *In Search of the Miraculous* by P. D. Ouspensky.
And there it was, way down on the bottom shelf near the wall,
lost among a motley grouping of unclassified mystical and
occult titles.

Again, it was rather late at night. I sat down in my armchair
under a warm cone of light, the rest of the house dark and quiet.
I wondered if the book would be anything like as electrifying
as it had been when I first read it years before. To tell the truth,
I did not expect much, even though the de Hartmann book
had made such a unique impression upon me. I had long since
"shelved" the Ouspensky book in my mind just as I had shelved
it along the wall.

From the very first pages, fragments of the whole teaching
began to come back to me. Man, said Gurdjieff, is actually not a
man, he is a machine—in whom and to whom everything simply
"happens." He can *do* nothing; he has no freedom of the will; he
lives in waking dreams and imagination. All the attributes of
man—freedom, understanding, love, creativity—are not his and
can never be his until he works for them. In short, man is asleep;
in sleep we live and in sleep we shall die, without ever having
awakened to what we are meant to be.

As I turned the pages, I also began remembering how I had
felt when I first read these things. It was not that I felt them anew;
I simply remembered how I had felt at the time. I remembered
my utter shock and disbelief, mirrored by how the author of

the book, Ouspensky himself, had felt in his first meetings with Gurdjieff in a noisy, smoky Moscow café. I especially remembered how I froze when I came across a passage[37] where Ouspensky listens to Gurdjieff saying that everything in the life of humanity—popular movements, wars, revolutions, changes of government—all this simply *happens.*

Ouspensky protests against the sweeping generalization that all people are mere machines. "There are savages," he says, "there are mechanized people, there are intellectual people, there are geniuses."

Gurdjieff replies: "Quite right, people are very unlike one another, but the real difference between people you do not know and cannot see. . . . All the people you see, all the people you know, all the people *you may get to know,* are machines working solely under the power of external influences. . . . Even now, at this very moment," says Gurdjieff, "several millions of machines are trying to annihilate one another. [World War I had begun]. . . . What is the difference between them? Where are the savages and where are the intellectuals? They are all alike. . . ."

About war and the possibility of ending war, Gurdjieff says, "If people were different everything would be different. They are what they are, so everything is as it is."

"This," writes Ouspensky, "was very difficult to swallow."

"Is there nothing, absolutely nothing that can be done?" he asks.

"Absolutely nothing," answers Gurdjieff.

I clearly remembered how those words stopped me.

Through all this, and much else besides, indicating the nearly hopeless human condition, Gurdjieff also speaks tellingly to Ouspensky about the possibility of escape from the prison of illusion and violence that dominates the life of humanity. I remembered my mixed emotions reading about the idea of an "ancient knowledge . . . distinct from our science and philosophy or even surpassing it." I remembered that I felt two things simultaneously: a thrill of hope and wonder, and at the same time a pronounced skepticism. This combination of emotions came often upon me as I read the book. As did the combination of terror and joy as I read what Gurdjieff said about death and immortality—that an immortal soul is a product of meticulously guided inner work, without which death is disappearance forever.

Now, many years later, I recognize and appreciate the significance of the simultaneous experience of two very distinct kinds of emotions, one of which was characterized by refusal and reaction and the other full of wordless affirmation and longing. But at my first reading of the book, I realized only that this book had the power of both troubling and calling to me as had no other book I had ever read. But as I have said, the figure of Gurdjieff himself as a man who spoke with unique authority carried me through even the most shocking ideas and startling metaphysical claims. When I now think of how that first acquaintance with the person of Gurdjieff struck me, I recognize that his way of behaving with Ouspensky had the same unique quality as the ideas themselves were having on me. And over the years I have observed the same fact in many of the accounts by people meeting and working with Gurdjieff. With one hand he drew people toward him while with the other hand, and with equal force, he pushed people away. This dual action had the effect of producing a unique inner opening in the psyche, a state in which a way opened within oneself leading toward an entirely new sense of one's own real being. Many who met Gurdjieff could not bear this experience.

I continued reading, more and more clearly remembering how the book had first struck me, more and more aware that I was holding fast to a certain "safe" distance from the book and from all my memories of how it had originally affected me. Torrents of new ideas about the structure of man and the structure of the universe were once again washing over me, a flood of ideas that years before had uprooted many of the assumptions and dearly held opinions that had at that time defined my intellectual identity. But half-consciously I was now saying to myself that I would not let that happen again.

I had just finished reading Ouspensky's account of what Gurdjieff called the state of "self-remembering." And once again, as had happened years before, I was trying to decipher what Ouspensky was talking about and why he gave it such importance. Remembering oneself? What could it mean? The phrase itself was odd and suggested very little to me, no matter how much I turned it over again and again in my mind.

The phrase is first introduced in the book when someone asks Gurdjieff about states of consciousness. In response, Gurdjieff says, among many other things, that human beings, as they are, have only the *possibility* of consciousness and, at best, only rare flashes of consciousness. I remembered how that statement also meant very little to me when I first read it. I had no idea at all how much hung on it, both concerning the integrity of Gurdjieff's ideas and in relation to the whole question of the meaning of human life itself and the definition of what a human being is meant to be.

The question of God was for me not yet in the picture at all.

Ouspensky then relates what he and his comrades experienced in the ongoing task of self-observation that they were given. After each person speaks, Gurdjieff admonishes them. "Not one of you has noticed that *you do not remember yourselves*. . . You do not feel *yourselves;* you are not conscious of *yourselves*. . .You do not feel: *I* observe, *I* notice, *I* see. Everything still 'is noticed,' 'is seen.' . . . In order really to observe oneself one must first of all *remember oneself.*"

He then tells them—and this once again struck me very forcibly and left me as puzzled as I was when I first read it: "Try to *remember yourselves* when you observe yourselves . . . Only those results will have any value that are accompanied by self-remembering. Otherwise you yourselves do not exist in your observations. In which case what are all your observations worth?"

Again I wondered: What could it mean, *"you yourselves do not exist"*? I had not encountered anything like that notion in all the Judaic, Christian, and Buddhist writings. On the contrary, wasn't the whole idea to become free of the sense of self? To erase one's personal identity and either merge with God or the universe or the "holy" Zen no-mind? Try as I might, I didn't notice, I didn't see in this idea of self-remembering what was there right in front of my eyes, something huge and totally central and yet totally invisible to me, like some great magic mountain. When the significance of this idea finally dawned on me years later, I nearly wept with wonder and shock that I could easily have gone through my whole life without knowing about it. I could have become a very successful professor or writer, perhaps famous and of great repute. And yet, it would have been as if I hadn't lived at all! Nor would I perhaps ever have been granted the understanding of how God could appear in human life. I would never have been touched by the power of hope that is brought by the fact that the question of God's existence and God's action in human life is very nearly identical with the question of whether or not, and to what degree, I myself exist!

CHAPTER SEVEN

Return to the Miraculous

As I continued reading, I was already beginning to sense myself in a new and yet strangely familiar way. I recognized—out of the corner of my eye—that as I read I was not being drawn toward the associations in my own mind. I was simply reading and "hearing" the words on the page—the equivalent of the rare moments when one listens to another person without at the same time being drawn into one's own thoughts: that is to say, when one listens to the words, not the "meaning" that one is automatically constructing out of the words. It is the very opposite of the degraded state of just reading or listening mechanically. No, this was neither the state of being drawn into one's own "insights" nor the state in which one comes to the end of a sentence or a page and suddenly realizes that there was no awareness at all of what had been read, that one had been dreaming while "it" was reading or "listening."

I was in the middle of the chapter following the discussion of self-remembering when an event occurred in me that ultimately led me to change the inner direction of my life.

In this particular chapter,[38] Gurdjieff is explaining to his pupils what he calls the fundamental laws which govern all processes both in the world and in man.

"The first fundamental law of the universe," he says, "is the law of three forces, or three principles, or, as it is often called, *the law of three,*" according to which "every action, every phenomenon in all worlds without exception, is the result of a simultaneous action of three forces—the positive, the negative and the neutralizing."

When this idea of the law of three had appeared earlier in the book, I found myself easily assimilating it into my familiarity with both Newtonian physics and the symbolism of the number three in fairy tales, mythology, and the religious doctrines of the world. The only thing that made me pause for a moment was when Gurdjieff had said that although the positive and negative forces may be apparent to ordinary observation (electricity, sexuality, etc.), the third force is invisible to human beings in the ordinary state of consciousness in which they live. But this aspect of the idea, the invisibility of the third force, was so strange to me that I simply parked it in my mind without wondering much about it at all.

In this particular chapter, however, it was the second fundamental law that was the main subject of discussion, and it was with regard to this law that something completely unexpected happened to me.

"The next fundamental law of the universe," says Gurdjieff, "is the *law of seven* or the *law of octaves.*" This law states that every developing process always and everywhere must of necessity pass through seven distinct stages before completion. This, he said, applies to all processes, whether it be vast cosmic phenomena, or the broad movements of human history and the defining events of one's own life, or the subtlest, most inner process within the individual human heart and soul.

The book here presents a rich account of many essential aspects of this idea, like an Oriental tapestry in which one is immediately struck by a bold and powerful central pattern which in turn leads the eye to lesser patterns within patterns, all filling out the central vision by endlessly adding new designs that constantly reawaken the attention.

Yet I remember at first simply saying to myself something like: Well, yes, here it is finally, the "magic number" seven. Doesn't every so-called occult doctrine sooner or later try to make something fantastic of it? A gentle, superficial wave of disappointment washed over me. But this reaction also I "parked" in my mind and went on, quietened, as I have said, by the straightforward words which somehow carried a current of authority and knowledge.

In this vibrantly sober state of mind, I continued to read with clear, relaxed attention and without further reactions of either affirmation or rejection. I read about the fundamental notion of the inherent discontinuity of all vibrations, a notion which contradicts Newton's first law of motion or inertia, which, roughly speaking, says that a body maintains its state of uniform motion unless acted upon by an external force. According to

Gurdjieff, on the contrary, all vibrations, and hence all individual movements of energy, intrinsically lose their force at certain precise stages in their development and therefore must receive an additional impulse of energy at certain stages or intervals in order to proceed in "a straight line," that is, in order to reach the aim or destination of the original impulse. Gurdjieff does make passing reference to certain of the newest theories in physics (this is in the year 1915) where the Newtonian law is beginning to be shaken, but, he says, "physics is still very far from a correct view of the nature of vibrations . . . in the real world."[39]

After developing this idea of the lawful discontinuity of vibrations, Gurdjieff states that "the laws which govern the retardation or the deflection of vibrations from their primary direction were known to ancient science," and "these laws were . . . incorporated into a particular formula . . . which has been preserved up to our times." This formula is the law of the octave, which comprises the eight stages in the development of vibrations as they pass from their initial state to their doubling (ascent) or to their diminishment by half (descent).

"In the guise of this formula," he says, "ideas of the octave have been handed down from teacher to pupil, from one school to another. In very remote times one of these schools found that it was possible to apply this formula to music. In this way was obtained the seven-tone musical scale which was known in the most distant antiquity, then forgotten, and then discovered or 'found' again."

He continues:

"At the same time, however, if we study the manifestations of the law of octaves in vibrations of other kinds we shall see that the laws are everywhere the same, and that light, heat, chemical, magnetic, and other vibrations are subject to the same laws as sound vibrations."

From this point on, through the formula as it is expressed in the diatonic musical scale, Gurdjieff lays forth a vision of the manner in which both world events and a man's own individual life either move toward a genuine aim or, on the contrary, go nowhere at all, repeating, repeating, endlessly, meaninglessly. . . .

Suddenly, I am looking at what at first seems on the page to be only an empty irregularly shaped geometric figure, a kind of asymmetric polygon. Startled, I had to turn back a few pages to understand what this diagram really meant. It suddenly seemed of great importance to me and I didn't know why. I understood the theoretical point of the diagram, but something was telling me that it had to do with *me*. With my *personal life*.

Slowly, I reread the preceding pages.

"If we grasp its full meaning," says Gurdjieff, "the law of octaves gives us an entirely new explanation of the whole of life, of the progress and development of phenomena on all planes of the universe observed by us. This law explains why there are no straight lines in nature and also why we can neither think nor do, why everything with us *is thought*, why everything *happens* with us and happens usually in a way opposed to what we want or expect. All this is the clear and direct effect of the 'intervals,' or retardations in the development of vibrations."

Using the terminology of the musical scale, Gurdjieff draws a short straight line, marking the successive points on the line as "do," "re," "mi." At this point the development of the octave has reached its first "interval," or retardation. And at this point, left to itself, without an additional influx of energy, a deviation takes place and the movement begins to change its initial direction. This change, or deflection, is indicated by continuing the line as it now angles downward, starting with the point indicated as the musical note "fa." Through fa, sol, la, and si the line continues, but the same deflection occurs at the si-do interval and the line descends at yet another angle and is now moving perpendicular to its original direction.

And so it continues, deflecting at each mi-fa and si-do interval of several octaves, tracing what is eventually a roughly circular path. Until, tracing the closed polygon, the line, says Gurdjieff, may return to its original direction. That is, the line may circle back to where it originally started!

"This law," he says, "shows why straight lines never occur in our activities, why, having begun to do one thing we in fact continually do something entirely different, often the opposite of the first, although we do not notice this and continue to think that we are doing the same thing that we began to do."

And now I am staring again at the irregular, empty polygon.

It is as if I am looking into a mirror at my own life.

No, it is more accurate to say that it *is* my whole life—not "as though." All my principal, recurring hopes and dreams, my expectations, my failures and disappointments, turning round again and again with the same, identical "taste"—with my ambitions to publish, my ambitions to excel, my attempts to achieve recognition, my yearning for meaningful relationships with women—everything that has taken place in both the broad daylight and the intimate nighttime of my life—all and everything was in an instant there in front of me in essence and full detail.

Without any warning at all, a column of intense, fine energy suddenly descends down the center of my body from my head to my abdomen. I am riveted to my chair, not knowing what to make of this column of vibrating energy, unlike anything I had ever experienced in my life.

So that was what this book was telling me! What this idea was telling me! All at once, the whole book took on a new meaning to me. Or, more precisely, the whole idea of the teaching took on a new meaning. I mean to say that I realized that until then I had been reading and seeing only the surface of the book and the teaching. And I saw, dimly but powerfully, that I had been living and thinking all these years only on the surface of my life and my mind.

All this was not in words, but in the blood and nerves of my being. Who was I? The question of Dr. Suzuki appeared again, but far more deeply. And who have I been all my life? Had all of my life been lived in a dream?

I wish to say that here, in this moment of writing these memories down, I am not writing "literature." I am staying as close as I can to bare facts. In all of this the idea of God was nowhere to be found—except . . . except my memories of this experience are all by themselves calling forth the experiences in my later life when there was no doubt at all that I was approaching that to which religion gives the name "God." What I am seeing now is that such experiences reside in a certain "place" within the psyche and there they reside forever. And there in that "place" certain related experiences gather together over the course of time. These experiences, and they are many and varied, gather together, associate together like countrymen, like family members, like lovers. They gather there and deepen each other. There they form as it were another life, another identity. There they, as it were, give form to the higher force-without-form that is the deeper Self which defines the essence of every human being. There, over much time, and with much powerful living, the second self is conceived and moves toward the moment of birth. This second self I have learned to think of as the real meaning of the word "soul." And the question I wish to open is—the wonderment I wish to open is: Is it only the soul of man that can say, in truth, "I am," "I exist"? And is it only the soul that can know and be known by that higher "something" that religion has called "God"? Heretical thought? Or the liberating, joyous truth that somehow and somewhere we have known all along?

We have known it.

I put down the book. I could read no further. Slowly, over many minutes, the energy lessened and distributed itself evenly throughout my whole body and then, over much time, slowly faded, as though having fed every cell in my body.

CHAPTER EIGHT

What Is a Human Being?

It is that family of experiences I wish now to speak about. One of my purposes is to show that nearly every human being has, at the very least, approached the experience of God, often without knowing it, without the means to understand the real significance of what he or she has experienced. Were people to understand even a little about this, the whole question of the existence of God would be transformed. There would no longer be either atheists who hotly deny the existence of God or cutthroat fundamentalists who deny anyone else's experience or belief but their own—and about whom it may be said that their own experience and belief are almost always fatally mixed with fantasy.

At the same time, I also wish to open further the essential question of the role of humanity itself in the life of the Earth and how that can lead toward a new definition of God. I wish to show that just as God's existence in one's own individual life depends upon the hidden question of whether or not I myself exist, so also does the possibility of the action of God in human history depend upon the level of being of mankind in general.

Begin by picturing a crowded street in downtown San Francisco. The year, I believe, is 1975. Late afternoon of a cool, cloudy November day, collars up, rain threatening. I am standing at the corner of Union Square with my great Tibetan friend, Lobsang Lhalungpa, waiting for the traffic light to change. That very day, and for a long time before that, my thoughts had been turning round and round about the Buddhist concept of the rarity of being born as a human being rather than as an animal or anything else. According to Buddhism, it is only human beings who have the possibility to escape from the great universal wheel of illusion—in human terms, the meaningless circle of repetition due to the continually deflecting, thwarted or displaced intentions of one's own personal life. The Buddhists illustrate this point by the image of a turtle swimming submerged in the great ocean, surfacing only once in a hundred years. We are told also to imagine an ox yoke floating somewhere on the surface of that ocean. What are the chances, we are asked, that when the turtle surfaces, his head will emerge right through the center of that ox yoke? That, they say, is how rare it is to have been born as a human being.

Standing there on the street corner with hundreds and thousands of people rushing by or crowding together, I blurted out my question. "Why, Lobsang," I said, "does Buddhism say it is so rare to be born as a human being? Look at all these people rushing around us—here and everywhere! It does not seem rare at all!" At first he only smiled that smile that felt like a butterfly gently appearing out of nowhere. The traffic light changed and we slowly crossed the street as people swarmed by us.

From the very first moment that I had met Lobsang Lhalungpa, some two years before, in the summer of 1973, I knew he was a remarkable human being—remarkable in the sense of *being*. The years that I had already spent trying to put into practice the Gurdjieff teaching had begun to sensitize me to the presence of this all-important, but nearly indefinable quality in certain people.

I had first come across his name preparing for a course I was about to teach. He had written a chapter in a book called *The Path of the Buddha*,[40] a collection of essays by Buddhist scholars representing the diverse interpretations of Buddhism that had developed over centuries throughout Asia. And although I had already read a great deal about Buddhism, especially Zen and Tibetan Buddhism, and had even written about it in my book *The New Religions,* Lobsang Lhalungpa's article, titled simply "Buddhism in Tibet," touched me as had no other by its clarity, simplicity and what I would now call its compassionate impartiality. No spiritual tradition anywhere is more complex, subtle, multilayered and profound than Tibetan Buddhism. Yet in this one learned summary, I felt I was glimpsing the essence not only of the Tibetan tradition, but of the whole of Buddhism in all its pure love and practical intelligence. Words on a page sometimes have the qualities of a living person, not only for all that they say, but for what they do not say in every sentence and paragraph. The long essay was full of a vast amount of information—historical, philosophical, spiritual. But the more it said, the more it did not say. The more it revealed about the teaching, the more it offered of restraint and silence.

This man was an incarnation of the qualities of his essay.

I met him in person under the following circumstances. I had been invited by the Gurdjieff Foundation of California to participate in a public lecture series entitled "Sacred Tradition and Present Need." I was asked to give the opening lecture and to help identify representatives of other spiritual traditions who could meaningfully confront the question of the lecture series, namely: How can or should the ancient traditions really help in a world that is so entirely different from the world in which these traditions had first appeared and in which they had developed over the passage of time? How could or should these ancient traditions speak to the man or woman of today who seems to have lost all ability to hear the sacred truths? In the end, an exceptional roster of speakers was assembled, which included Father William Johnston and Dom Aelred Graham, representing Christianity; Seyyed Hossein Nasr, representing the Sufi tradition within Islam; P. L. Travers, speaking from within the world of ancient myth—and several other equally distinguished but lesser known men and women. Lobsang Lhalungpa had been one of these people.[41]

But it was only a few years after the lecture series that I really came to know him. Once again, it was on the initiative of the

Gurdjieff Foundation, under the direction of John Pentland, the man who had become like a second father to me. The idea was to translate into plain English *The Life of Milarepa,*[42] the most beloved book and story from within the Tibetan Buddhist tradition. Personally speaking, if I had to recommend one book that gives the essence of Buddhist spirituality, it would be this one. No more joyous and terrifying book can be found anywhere—terrifying in what it demonstrates to be a life without genuine inner work on oneself, and joyous in the depiction not only of the taste of inner freedom, but of the love that has for centuries been pouring out toward mankind from extraordinary men and women who have worked on themselves for the sake of humanity. It is a book, as Milarepa himself says, full of laughter and tears, a dramatic story that can never be forgotten. Lobsang Lhalungpa, who at that time was living with his family in Seattle, came down to San Francisco about once a month to work with our small team of "translators."

I put "translators" in quotation marks because obviously it was only Lobsang who knew the Tibetan language. The rest of us were simply there to try to find the most apt English phrasing of what he translated. Here I must say something about what our translating work was meant for. As in everything undertaken by students of the Gurdjieff teaching, the fundamental aim of working together at anything—in this case at translating important texts—was to see ourselves as we are and to try to open ourselves to what I have already referred to as the experience of self-remembering. That was the inner aim. And in the process, our little team, consisting of a few elderly ladies and a middle-aged professor, feasted every week on impressions of our egoism as we tried to convince each other that our understanding of the wording of a sentence was the only possible one.

But when Lobsang was there, we were continually shocked by his equanimity, his gentle, butterfly smile, and the soft bird-like trilling of his voice every time any one of us self-assertively put forward our "great understanding" of the meaning of the text. "Ooooo," he would melodically say, agreeing with everyone and everything, even though he was obviously the only person there who really understood the Tibetan words and the Buddhist meaning of the sentence or word in question. As a result, every-one mysteriously felt that he or she was "right," even though there was usually nothing but sharp disagreement among all of us. And somehow, the right translation would appear after many raised voices on our part and many lovely *ooooo*s on Lobsang's part. Of course, each time in this process it was Lobsang's under-standing of the correct meaning that found its way onto the page. And we all came away feeling that we had been, if not right, then at least instrumental in solving every problem. In short, he embodied inner calm and freedom from attachment in a matter—the presentation of the Tibetan tradition to the Western world—that was as important to him as his life's blood and to which he was, in fact, devoting his life.

The quality and strength of Lobsang's inner being was also

brought home to me through an event that took place in my home. After one of his weekends working with our translation group, he stayed for a few days as a guest in my house in San Francisco. One morning at the breakfast table we were discussing this and that, I don't remember what. My nine-year-old daughter, Eve, was present. Ordinarily, she tended to be shy, especially when strangers or guests were present. But at one point in the conversation, during a brief pause, she looked up at Lobsang and without any preamble she asked him: "What happens when people die?"

I was startled and a certain warmth rose up in me. It was obvious she had been keeping this question for a long time inside herself, without letting anyone know. My own attempts to make room in our relationship for this kind of question had not gone anywhere, or so it had seemed to me. But now, suddenly, I felt her hidden self and felt the strength of its need. How would Lobsang respond? I set myself to listen to him with as much eagerness as my daughter.

Lobsang turned toward her with his warm, brown face and his lucent black eyes and began talking to her as though she were, like him, simply a normal human being for whom such questioning was as natural and important as eating, a human being who was, like him and like all of us, someday going to die. I don't remember the content of what he said to her; I do remember thinking that what he said was not extraordinary— things that any serious adult might say to a serious, inquiring child. But what I do remember as vividly as though it were yesterday was the "resonance" of his voice, the stillness of his body and the warm attention in his face. I remember sensing the vibration of a certain kind of energy passing between him and my daughter. I saw her posture become firm. Her own attention deepened and quietened. I realized that something was passing between Lobsang and my daughter that served more as answer to her question than any words by themselves could have. I saw her eyes deepen as though they were seeing something strong and new—not outside herself, but inside herself.

Perhaps she did not realize what was happening inside herself. Maybe she still doesn't know. But I saw it. A quality of attention was passing between Lobsang and my daughter that is becoming more and more rare in our common world. And it is this "something" that desperately needs to pass between people. It is the mutual flow of this special quality of attention between human beings that all people, whether they know it or not, are starved for. Not all the praise, touching, words, teaching, smiling, sympathizing, serving good causes—not any or all of it can do what this quality of shared attention can do. Its lack is more of a threat to our world than anything else—or, rather, its increasing absence in human relationships is at the root of all else that now threatens to destroy or degrade us beyond recovery—the internecine hatred and egoism and immorality that is crowding out not only ancient, traditional ways of life, and the life of nature itself, but which is also crowding out the human memory of what mankind is and is made for.

We are back in Union Square in downtown San Francisco. Lobsang and I have crossed the street. I stop our walking for a moment and repeat my question, this time a bit insistently. "Look at all these people," I say to him. "Just look! How can you say that it is rare to be born as a human being?"

The wind is picking up. A few raindrops in the air. Would all he would give me again be only silence and his butterfly smile?

Nothing like that. His face was uncharacteristically sober, almost stern. He raised his hand halfway out toward the crowds.

"How many human beings do you see?"

For a long moment I simply looked at him.

CHAPTER NINE

And What of God?

It is astonishing to me to realize how long it took me to see the connection between the experience of remembering myself and the question of the existence of God. And for this I am now profoundly grateful. Had I glimpsed this fundamental connection too soon, I would almost surely have mixed them up together, which would perhaps have put an end to my ability to profit from the help being offered to me by the ideas and friendships that were supporting my inner search. I will try to explain this apparent paradox soon.

For now I simply have to hew to what was actually taking place in my life at that time and what it entails about the meaning of the idea of God.

Even as my appreciation of the mystical teachings of religion deepened and my experience of how a momentary contact with "I am" transformed everything in me, including my relationship to others and to the world—even so, I made no connection between these two currents of my life. I did not see at all that everything that historically has been part of the idea of God, how all of what have been called the divine attributes of God—power, justice, mercy, etc.—were actually, at their own level and scale, attributes of the deeper self, or attention, that was more and more often touching me.

I speak of this now, in this book, not because of its significance for me personally, but because of its possible significance for others—dare I say more than that? How much of the sorrow and grief of the world lies in what we have made of the idea of God and what, in the name of God, we believe is demanded of us! How much bitter egoism with all its violence and inhumanity has been played out on a massive scale—the scale of whole nations and peoples, whole historical epochs—because of mankind's crippled relationship to the idea of whatever is called God in our lives! And how much grief and sorrow has, in its turn, also arisen because of a set of mind and the disillusioned heart that leads a man or woman to turn away entirely from the possible influence, in one's life and behavior, of what is immeasurably higher both above and within ourselves! How many worlds have fallen to pieces in our personal lives and in the life of humanity because individually and collectively, mankind has turned for guidance to that which is incapable of the whole-being-intelligence which alone can put all our capacities to the service of what is good—because we have turned to what only pretends to be higher in ourselves? And that which pretends to be God or a higher authority in or above ourselves: Is it not only our mental automatisms or emotional uprisings or fantastic moralistic dreams—dreams spun out of the lonely ego as it manipulates the world with technologies that amplify our fears and cravings?

Messages

Every relatively normal man, woman or child has genuine experiences of the inner world of the Self. But in a culture such as our own, these experiences are not recognized as what in fact they are: namely, "messages" from the Self indicating what a human being is meant to be and what he or she can become. These experiences are often simply set aside as accidental gifts or "peak experiences," and nothing more. Or perhaps they are linked with specific religious beliefs without the necessary practical guidance that may have once been available in more traditional cultures. Rarely is their immense significance understood as a sign that we are not what we think we are. Rarely are they "heard" as a call rather than as an "answer."

A call to . . . what?

Inner Empiricism

Here we face a difficulty of language. How to speak honestly about this specific quality of inner experience and the knowledge it brings? Immediately to put labels on it—such as "mysticism," "inspiration," "transpersonal insight"—is to throw down an impassable obstacle to seeing it for what it is. And I say this as one who has studied mystical religious texts with both reverence and scholarly care, and with my best efforts of logical and philosophical critical analysis. Equally, to relegate such experience to the realm of "religious faith" or "inspiration" or "intuition" is also fatally misleading if we take these words as they are conventionally understood. Even to use the word "knowledge" can draw us away from grasping what is essential about the experience of "I am." And the reason is that the knowledge that this experience can bring is immeasurably different in nature and quality from what we call by that word. And yet, once such experience is seen for what it is, such knowledge and how it acts in us bids fair to answer the dream of knowledge that has called to man from the beginning of time—a dream, a hope, an aspiration that has also, in its own way, specifically defined the genius of our modern world: the aim of knowing reality, and in the light of such knowledge, working to perfect ourselves and our common life.

Let me put the point simply and bluntly. Science demands that we base all our knowledge upon actual experience, but it denies the validity and even the existence of objective inner experience that yields knowledge of the real world. It strictly limits the possibility of obtaining knowledge about nature and about the universe to data received through sense perceptions—sight, hearing, taste, etc.—which in their turn are organized by the mind into concepts and theories that then require further sense perceptions for their validation. This point of view about knowledge is known as empiricism, derived from the Greek word for "experience," *empeiria*. Defined most generally, the doctrine of empiricism tells us that all knowledge must be rooted and tested by actual observation of events and objects in the external world. According to this doctrine, the power of reason or thought alone, without the content of actual observation, actual experience, can yield only logical, formal structures that are empty of factual content. This doctrine of empiricism—putting the matter in its simplest terms—forms the very heart and backbone of the modern, scientific era in which all of our lives have been immersed for centuries.

Again, putting the matter simply, this doctrine overlooks or is ignorant of a massive, towering fact—namely, the existence of the *discipline of inner experience*, experience of the inner world that is as precise and undeniable as the facts brought to light by sensory experience of the external world and organized into systematic theory by mathematics and logic. That is to say: science, in all its power and authority, is based solely on what we may call external empiricism. It knows little or nothing about what we may therefore call *inner empiricism*. Yes, modern thought recognizes what is called "religious experience." But it tends to lump all such accounts of religious experience together as mere subjective events which offer little or no objective knowledge of objective reality.

The fundamental teachings of the great spiritual traditions and spiritual philosophies of the world are rooted in the disciplined work of inner empiricism. Through inner empiricism, knowledge about the universe and man is obtained of a kind and with a content that is inaccessible to modern science.

The existence of inner empiricism has become invisible to science and our modern world partly because many religiously or metaphysically oriented teachings either have pretended to have such higher knowledge or were promulgated by individuals who themselves were unaware, sometimes willfully and arrogantly, of the conditions of life and struggle that were necessary for genuine inner knowledge. These pretensions have for centuries been, often rightly, exposed as empty fantasies, leading more and more to the feeling of certainty among scientifically trained minds that there is no such thing as higher, inner knowledge. As one insightful observer has put it, "It is probably impossible for someone who hasn't actually explored the possibilities inherent in 'inner knowledge' to accept this kind of knowledge, and not to suspect it or reject it as being magical, irrational, primitive, emotional, or whatever."[43]

But such knowledge exists. In the vast realm of the inner world of man there exists, in miniature as it were, the entire great world around and above us, the entire universal order. The dominance of the school of external empiricism is based on the assumption that man is only a tiny fragment of the whole of nature and the universal world. But what if it were otherwise? What if human beings are in some real sense unique creations containing in their essential being all the laws and elements, all the forces and energies—from the most conscious to the most inert—that are at play in the great universe? If that were so, then self-knowledge would be—could be—far, far more than information about our psychological moods, emotions, memories, thoughts and behavior. Self-knowledge would be far more than the results of looking at ourselves from "outside," as it were—that is, from our everyday conceptual mind by which we try to organize the world as it is received by our senses. If a human being were really, as it was understood in very ancient times, a microcosm, a miniature universe, then self-knowledge not only would be the knowledge of reality so longed for in the hopes and dreams of science, but also could be a means itself of inner self-creation—inner self-creation parallel in its way to the creation of worlds that takes place in the universe itself.

The universe? From where did it come? How? When? By what energies did what we see only in tiny glimpses come into being?—the universe containing infinities of organized, living worlds, earths, suns, galaxies—cells, organic life, atmosphere—purpose, directions, and lawful order, fundamental forces at work everywhere and in everything—all of which emerged out of what? By what greater mind? By what intelligence did it all appear, an intelligence that embraces even the automatisms of Darwinian evolution on the ground of which everything from a mosquito to a Buddha appears on this earth? In such a case, self-knowledge and experience would not be a passive recording for manipulation of impressions from without, but a seminal generation of realities within realities—just as in any organism the *telos* or purpose of the whole generates the elements and organs and instrumentalities that maintain the inner world of the organism. And man? Of all creatures we know of on Earth, the intelligent self-regulating and self-creating force would have the added attribute that completes the structure of the universe we know—and that added attribute is conscious intelligence, consciousness as a force of nature, a universal energy. Who, looking at "the starry sky above and the moral law within" can really maintain that it all "just happened"?

No, such knowledge exists. Not only does it bring us facts of an entirely different nature and scale than can be brought by external empiricism, external experience, but such knowledge also is and can become a force of self-creation by which worlds are born and live and die—and among such worlds are we human beings, such as we are meant to be.

We need a new language, or perhaps the old language carrying a new current of being, in order to begin to understand the experiences that are granted us all as human beings, experiences that need to be cultivated, intentionally and precisely, in order to serve as a force not only for self-knowledge but for self-transformation. We know there are experiences that transform us in a moment—moments that are then forgotten or that depend on infrequent accident. But what if we could become more available to such experiences, live in a way that could invite them more into our lives?

What if we could, in Gurdjieff's words, remember ourselves always and everywhere?

The question remains: There exist in our lives experiences of oneself that need to be understood as a call. But a call . . . to what? And a call *from* what?

CHAPTER TEN

The Critique of Pure Reason

There is a heavy, dog-eared book on the desk in front of me. On the torn spine the title still carries the power it held for me over fifty years ago.

Kant's *Critique of Pure Reason*.

Even now, holding it in my hand, I feel a sensation of warmth, like meeting an old friend or enemy with whom years of mingled love and fear once defined one's life. Years of intensely vivid struggle, hope and despair—years that one treasures for the intensity of living that they brought, quite apart from the actual triumphs or defeats associated with them which are now of secondary importance.

But the intensity—ah! I was in my second year at college, still pinching myself as I walked through Harvard Yard, basking in amazement that I was actually here in this legendary place with its aura of history, privilege, great learning, great wealth—gentile, Christian New England America. I, Jerry Needleman, a little Jewish kid from a lower-middle-class family of immigrant grandparents.

I was eighteen years old. My dreams of a life in science and medicine were already yielding to the allure of philosophy. I was becoming dimly aware that what I loved about science, especially biology, was that it showed me reality, nature, as a world of ideas. Life, and all living things, were *ideas*—units of meaning and purpose incarnated in matter that one could touch and hold—and work to *understand*. Dimly, very dimly, I was becoming aware that the study of nature also called me to a part of myself that I loved—*and that loved me!*

Yes, I loved nature and living things—the life in my father's garden, the star-filled sky, the splayed frog on my high school dissecting table and Mr. Boris's lucid explanations.

And I choked with tears studying the proofs in Euclidean geometry: Out of a mere handful of self-evident axioms, through the logic that was inherent in consciousness, the forms of the great world emerged, co-created by my own joyous efforts of attentive thought! Mr. Maclasky, with your necktie askew and your shirttail hanging out, did you know that you were showing us the bones of God? And Mr. Goldman, Samuel Goldman, unlit cigar in your hand; shiny, domed head; complaining about all human stupidity; suited like a movie gangster: Were you aware that your explanations of such things as how to balance chemical equations made us feel that the material world we lived in, the water, the wood, the metal, the food we ate, our bodies themselves, were all composed not merely of invisible atoms and molecules but also, and even more so, of mind, the very kind of laws that we were discovering in the structure of our own powers of thought?

Or were these first teachers of mine as unaware as I was that their work was inseminating something in man, something in myself that touched me and called to me like nothing else in my life—not any of my desires, fears, ambitions, hopes, pleasures, fantasies and daydreams? Something in myself, in oneself, that is fed not by praise or success or pleasure or revenge or . . . ? Something that *cared for me* far more than I could understand or intentionally work to care for *it*?

But all this, and much else besides in a normally precocious intellectual adolescence, seemed now, for a season, to be only preparation for the encounter with Immanuel Kant's *Critique of Pure Reason.*

The professor was a newly hired young man named Roderick Firth. I remember nothing about him personally except for his clear complexion and, for some reason, his eyeglasses that reflected flashes of light all the time. And I remember him blandly assigning us to read *The Critique of Pure Reason* in six weeks, at the end of which time we would be tested and graded.

Six weeks, I naïvely thought to myself, what a lot of time!

From all my previous random reading of philosophy as a teenager, I understood only that Kant (1724–1804) was generally considered the most important philosopher of the modern era, and perhaps, according to some, of all time. He was pictured as a little man with a huge mind who never once in all his long life ventured more than a few steps away from his native town of Königsberg in northern Germany. And yet, so I had read, the thought of this apparently timid little professor, and this one book in particular, immediately struck like lightning through all of Europe and shook the world. And still shakes the world.

Kant himself compared his philosophy to the revolutionary vision of the sixteenth-century Polish astronomer and priest Nicolaus Copernicus (1473–1543). As every schoolchild learns, or used to learn, Copernicus tore down the accepted view of the place of the Earth in the universe.Up to the time of Copernicus, so the story goes, it seemed obvious that the sun moved in the sky, circling around the stationary Earth. But Copernicus introduced a radically different idea. It was, he said, the Earth that moved, creating the appearance of the movement of the sun.

Similarly, up to the time of Kant it seemed obvious that to know something meant that in some way thought conformed to or mirrored the thing known. Just as a good mirror does not change the image of the object it mirrors, so knowledge is true to the extent that, like a good mirror, it simply reflects or describes the real object as it is "out there." But, like Copernicus, Kant introduced a radically different view. For Kant, it was, so to say, the "movement" of the mind itself—the fundamental laws governing the process of thought—that shaped, rather than simply reflected, the basic structure of things as they came to be known. The mind was not a mirror, it was a kind of "sculptor," shaping the fundamental lineaments of reality in the process of perception.

For centuries the geocentric picture of the cosmos had held sway, and all the apparent movements of the sun and planets were described by various complex circular motions with the Earth at the center. Copernicus showed that it was mathematically much simpler, and therefore truer, to regard the sun as the center of what we now call the solar system. After Copernicus, the Earth was soon understood to be but one of several planets orbiting the sun. All the motions and revolutions of the planets were viewed, as they now are, as revolutions around the sun, which itself was taken in this model as stationary.

The Copernican Revolution has had enormous implications with respect not only to science but to mankind's collective ego. No longer was man's home, the Earth, as cosmically important as the Church had assumed. Of course, the entire modern picture of the universe represents an immense development of the Copernican Revolution. Not only the Earth, but the sun and the solar system itself, and even our unimaginably vast galaxy, are now understood as small elements in the endless, evolving universe.

Such in simple terms is and was the impact of the Copernican Revolution. And, in a way that was even more telling and startling, such was and is the impact of Kant's philosophy. The general message of Kant's book is clear. Just as what had seemed to be the movement of the heavenly bodies around the Earth was actually an "appearance" created by the movement of the Earth itself, so also what seemed to be the real world that presented itself to the human mind was actually not the real world at all! The real world, reality itself defined as that which exists in and for itself, independent of whether or not we know it—this real world, the world of things in themselves, is forever veiled from us. We can never know reality because in the very act of knowing, human reason structures the world according to the fundamental laws of its own functioning. We can only know *appearances,* that is, the world as it appears to us after being generally organized by the mind. Like the planet Earth circling the sun and imagining, so to say, that the sun is moving around it, the human mind imagines it is obtaining certainty about the real world when in fact it is only imposing its own rational functioning upon a reality that it can never really see. The indisputable knowledge we have of the world is only indisputable because we have projected our own logic upon it. In knowing the world, we actually "create" it in its most fundamental structure.

For the last three hundred years this insight of Kant, in many and various colorations, has acted like an immense intellectual volcano affecting the entire landscape of our modern world's understanding of what we can and cannot know. So much I had more or less understood about Kant without ever having studied or tried to read or even held in my hands this heavy, dark red book, *The Critique of Pure Reason.* I knew nothing about the real basis of this Kantian view; I knew nothing of the subtleties and complexities of his arguments. I knew very little of the historical and philosophical background. From my previous readings and from the courses I had taken in my freshman year, I was acquainted with the distinction between two fundamental kinds of knowing—*a priori* knowledge and *a posteriori* knowledge—a distinction that has generated tremendous dynamism and controversy in the whole of the modern world's view of human knowledge. But I really had no idea that this distinction between knowledge attained by the thought alone and knowledge rooted in sensory experience would, in Kant's hands, in one gigantic, sustained argument at the heart of this book, overturn all possible belief in the existence of God. I only "knew" from all that I had up till then read about Kant that this book would completely and irrefutably justify my at that time already passionately held atheism.

And so I wasted no time tackling the book only minutes after buying it.

It was an indescribably beautiful September morning. I remember impatiently striding under the glorious trees in Harvard Yard and sitting down on the broad steps of Harvard's awe-inspiring Widener Library with its massive columns standing like ancestors above and behind me. Across the leafy Yard I was looking at none other than the main religious building of the Harvard campus, Memorial Church, with its own columns, which to me had a vapidly smooth white sheen that made them seem more ornamental than structural and certainly in no way comparable to the towering stone pillars holding up the entrance to the temple of learning behind me.

I looked down and opened *The Critique of Pure Reason*.

All that I had heard about the greatness of this book, including its reputation of being immensely difficult to understand, warmed me as much as the September sun. I couldn't have felt happier.

The very first sentence thrilled me:

Human reason has this peculiar fate that in one species of its knowledge it is burdened by questions which, as prescribed by the very nature of reason itself, it is not able to ignore, but which, as transcending all its powers, it is also not able to answer.[44]

I immediately closed the book. I almost wept. I sat there trembling, so touched that I was unable to read further. I felt not so much that I had found something I was looking for all my short life, but that this something had found me.

I know this may sound romantic or excessive or adolescent.

And it is here that the problem of language—or something mysteriously related to the problem of language—rears its head. How to explain the powerful sense of homecoming that this one sentence called forth in me? Even now, more than half a century later, I can find no words to explain this sensation, this deep intuition. I can only resort to a certain definite experience that many of us will recognize, but which may seem odd or farfetched as an analogy to what I then experienced reading this almost prosaic philosophical sentence in this mammoth, abstract philosophical text dealing with the limits of human knowledge.

Many of us can clearly remember the experience of falling in love at first sight. Not simply immediate attraction, physical or otherwise. I mean the experience of seeing and meeting the one great love of one's life.

Perhaps he or she walks into a room or you are introduced to her at some social event or you see him, whom you have known for many years but whom you now see as though for the first time. And you know—you *know*—that this man or woman is the one you have been looking for, perhaps without even being aware that you were longing for him or her.

Reading this sentence, and feeling the great weight of this book in my hands, was very much akin to that experience.

There are many love stories in the literature of nations that exist at several levels, love stories that are symbolic of man's relationship to God. Some are tragedies, such as the story of Tristan and Isolde or, in its way, Romeo and Juliet, but even when they are tragic, or perhaps especially when they are tragic, they evoke a certain mysterious joy because they are at one level stories of man's encounter with the Higher in one's self and in one's life, an encounter that destroys the everyday values of one's everyday life; a love that risks everything that the hero and heroine have till then considered important—social values, achievements, status, success, wealth, pleasure, safety, legacy— in short, a man or woman's ordinary identity, ordinary state of consciousness and sense of self. The hero or heroine sacrifices it all, throws himself or herself away, so to say, for the sake of this great love, even to the point of dying for the sake of this love, whether or not it is consummated. The writings of the Sufis are full of such stories—read almost any poem or tale by Rumi, Hafiz, or Mirabai.

The Hebraic tradition is also replete with such imagery, the Song of Solomon being the best-known example. But one finds this same imagery in the literature of Hasidism. There the imagery offers itself as more than imagery. It offers itself as explaining real flesh-and-blood life experience between a man and a woman. This it does by bringing a powerful metaphysical context to the experience of falling deeply in love, with one's whole being. In these stories, or explanations, the loved one had existed in another dimension ("heaven"), waiting to be born in order for the lovers to find their way toward each other. Tales such as this mirror the experience of real life, and for those who have been touched by such love, these tales are more than fiction. And at the same time they are more than so-called real, but actually not-so-real life. Such love makes so-called "reality" just that—*so-called*, that is to say, unreal, mixed with illusion and mere appearance, and holding no essential happiness: the happiness that in fairy tales symbolizes the joy of discovering what is called God, or the higher and most real purpose of one's life.

These are tales of God—Sufi, Christian, Judaic, Hindu, Buddhist. This imagery exists in almost every tradition, because this idea of God exists in almost every tradition, whether or not it is called God or the Absolute or—as in Buddhism or as it is in the Gurdjieff teaching—*consciousness* in its higher levels.

These are moments when the future meets us, finds us. Perhaps that is one meaning of the idea of fate or destiny. But this idea is deeper than its sometimes merely abstract presentation—outside of a story or myth, the artistry of which evokes the feeling of profound wonder. The future comes to meet us—and here the future is another word for one's true being, for Truth with a capital T. And woe to him or her who turns away from it.

With all the success or pleasure that ordinary values may bring, a man or woman will never experience the real purpose of human life.

There are moments, that is, of awakening in a world and in a life where nearly everything conspires to put one back to sleep. This question, this idea so simply expressed by Kant and with such sureness—a sureness that can only be the result of tremendous efforts of thought and work—this question came to me both from my past childhood and from my future adulthood. It came not just as an intriguing philosophical "issue"—I can cite many such "problems of philosophy," which may be intellectually very interesting, but which for me do not carry the authority or magic of this question. No, this question came with higher "credentials"—and I could tell many stories from many lands about these credentials, about man being sought out by Truth and called to strive for it, to embrace it, to marry it.

Sitting there on the steps of Widener Library, I was almost afraid to read further.

CHAPTER ELEVEN

Echo from the Future

In the autumn sun, sitting on the stone steps of Widener Library, the budding young philosopher had no interest in the intellectual history or cultural conditions within which the book in his hands was originally written. I was in love with *knowing*; in love with *understanding*, and nothing else. Only later did I begin to realize that this love of knowing was rooted in the love of freedom, the yearning for freedom. Freedom of the mind. But these words, "freedom of the mind," may not really convey what was and is at stake. It is human freedom itself that is at stake, the essence of what it means to be Man, a human being.

I kept the book closed with my finger on the first page.

Perhaps I should have been thinking about the philosophical issues that prompted Kant to write his book. But I don't remember thinking about any of that. I'm sure Professor Firth must have prepared us for Kant's *Critique* by explaining the philosophical controversy that existed at that time (and still exists) between the "rationalists," those who believed that reality can be known by means of the mind alone, and the "empiricists," who claimed that the only basis of knowledge is sensory experience of the external world. And I do clearly remember that the distinction between these two kinds of knowing was designated by the Latin phrases *a priori* and *a posteriori*. The former referred to knowledge that is "prior to"—that is, independent of—experience, and the latter referred to knowledge that is dependent upon, "posterior," to experience. I'm sure Professor Firth had told us that this distinction was essential to understanding Kant's great book, and I'm sure he went into considerable detail explaining it. In fact, that distinction and those Latin words would soon loom large in my mind, and eventually they would play a tremendous role in my realization of the vastness of what a human being actually can know, with certainty, about God. However, that came much later in my life.

But then and there: Who really cared about any of that? At that moment in Harvard Yard, just that one first sentence of Kant's book eclipsed everything else. Perhaps, mysteriously, I was hearing in that one sentence an echo from the future coming to meet me, as several years later I was to be touched by the same thought written in almost the same words by Dr. Suzuki.[45] And even more dramatically when I learned from my own years of inner work that the great questions of life cannot be answered by the mind alone, but only when they are asked with the whole of one's being. Perhaps I was so drawn to that statement by Kant because it called to my metaphysical subconscious where the "I am" was also calling to me.

Perhaps.

In any case, I'm sure that the good Professor Firth, his eyeglasses flashing, had told us what had electrified Kant's own mind, compelling him to confront the stark contradiction between, on the one hand, knowledge about the world that is certain and irrefutable and, on the other hand, the *impossibility of certainty* about the world as it is in itself—the *impossibility of certainty* about where things came from, where they are going; about the ultimate structure of matter, about the nature and destiny of the human soul and, above all, about what God is and whether God exists at all.

Many leading thinkers of Kant's time offered powerful visions of the ultimate structure and origins of the universe and about God and human destiny. Such thinkers were called *metaphysicians* and they traced their lineage back over the course of thousands of years to the greatest philosophers of the ancient world—especially to Plato and Aristotle, the honored luminaries of ancient Greece. Kant himself, it would seem, had also identified his own intellectual work as metaphysics. *Metaphysics:* the science dealing with ultimate reality, with the real world as it is in itself, apart from anything we or anyone may think about it: the world of God and His creation. *Metaphysics:* the queen of the sciences! Metaphysics: lying at the deep root of all the great questions of the human heart!

But then, so the good Professor Firth must have told us, along came David Hume!

The story of the stunning influence upon Kant of this brilliant young Scottish philosopher, Hume, has by now taken on the aura of legend, philosophical legend. Were one to cast it as an actual myth, Hume might be costumed as the mythic Hermes, the eternally young god of the crossroads, the god of turning points, at one and the same time thief, trickster, bearer of Higher Truth, who removes from us our seemingly precious garments of opinion and self-image in order to liberate the human soul.

It was the youthful Hume, the most radical, the most severely honest, of empiricists, who looked directly into his own mind and realized that *he could observe no such thing as the self.*

"For my part," he writes,

> *when I enter most intimately into what I call* myself, *I always stumble on some particular perception or other, of heat or cold, light or shade, love or hatred, pain or pleasure. I never can catch* myself *at any time without a perception, and never can observe anything but the perception. When my perceptions are removed for any time, as by sound sleep, so long am I insensible of* myself, *and may truly be said not to exist.*[46]

In one bold stroke, supported before and after by exquisite logic and argument, Hume, the honest empiricist, exposes and destroys the most universal and intimate illusion of humanity—the belief in the reality of one's own self! What could be more shattering to the mind?

Was it really true that we actually have never genuinely experienced the self that we are? And therefore, applying Hume's words, can it not be said that we—I, "myself"—do not actually exist? Had Hume discovered, if only in his mind, the hidden question-within-the-question of *Who am I?*—namely, the question of whether I myself exist at all?

Similar thoughts about the illusion of selfhood, in a much riper form, have of course been common in the spiritual traditions of the world, but it is doubtful that Kant had much acquaintance with the teachings of the Buddhists and the Hindus. And in any case, this argument about the illusion of the self—*my* self—was here being presented not by a mystic shrouded in antique, sacred language, but by one of the most fiercely contemporary and clear-minded men of his time.

But for Kant this would not have been the worst of it. Hume went even further with his seemingly never-before-so-radical empiricism. There is also no such thing, says Hume, as *causality*!

Just look and see, says Hume, look and see what it is that you call causes and their effects. Look, observe, separate yourself for a moment from your ingrained beliefs. Do you ever actually see, ever actually *experience* a force that acts as a cause in the world you see? The answer is no.

The answer is no. The idea of causation, says Hume very sensibly, involves the idea of an apparently necessary connection between events or experiences. When we say that A causes B, writes Hume, all we are really saying is that, so far, when B (whatever it is) has happened, then A has been present or has preceded it. The idea of *causation* simply refers to the habitual juxtaposition of two types of events or experiences.

We tend to think of causation as involving a force that makes something happen. But all we really *observe* is that one kind of experience or event has so far never occurred without being preceded or accompanied by a certain specific other kind of experience or event. We never observe a *force* that makes the experience or event take place.

The long and the short of it was that there can be no certain knowledge about the world we live in. To be certain about anything means that denying it would be a logical contradiction equivalent to claiming that two plus two equals five. The point is that no matter how many times we observe, for example, that thunder is preceded or accompanied by lightning, we cannot say with *certainty* that lightning causes thunder! All we can honestly say is that, so far, every time we have experienced the event of thunder (B), it has been preceded or accompanied by lightning (A). But there is no certainty here, no necessary connection between A and B, no *logical contradiction* involved in the thought that thunder is not caused by lightning.

Has the entire edifice of human knowledge been undone? The idea of causality lies at the deepest root of all that humanity calls knowledge. And this root does not exist? It is not there?

Look through all the books in all the libraries of the world, says Hume. Take in your hands any volume dealing with God or metaphysics, and, he says,

Let us ask: Does it contain any abstract reasoning concerning quantity or number? No. Does it contain any

experimental reasoning concerning matter of fact and existence? No.

That is, does the book contain logical certainties? Or reasoning based on actual empirical observation? The answer to both questions is no, it does not.

Therefore, Hume concludes:

Commit it then to the flames, for it can contain nothing but sophistry and illusion.[47]

We do not actually know when Kant learned of Hume's early arguments about the self. What we do know is that Kant could neither accept nor reject Hume's view about causality and what that view implied: namely, that there can never be certainty in our knowledge of the world. Thus, it was not Hume's denial of the existence of the self that awakened Kant from his "dogmatic slumber." What awakened Kant was Hume's denial of the universal law of causality and what that denial implied concerning the impossibility of certainty. It was Hume's empirical argument leading to that denial that Kant found both irrefutable and yet utterly unacceptable. Had not Isaac Newton discovered ironclad laws governing the universe—from the planets orbiting the sun to the apple falling from the tree? Was there not arising in the world a great new tide of scientific knowledge, where at last humanity could know the truths about nature, rather than blindly believing in this or that piece of homespun information about the physical and biological world—information, as often as not, stitched carelessly into the fabric of dogmatic religious or metaphysical beliefs?

For Kant, Reason was akin to God—at least that is what I felt even without reading more than a sentence of his great book. There had to be Truth. It could not be otherwise.

Here, however, it is necessary to be especially clear about what Kant means by the word "Reason." Otherwise he might be taken as just one more "Eurocentric" thinker, ignoring the psychological and philosophical diversity of the global world we live in, with its many culturally unique peoples.

Kant is speaking about something that he took to define what it means to be human. He is speaking about inner freedom, the intrinsic freedom of the human soul. Nothing which we in our contemporary world have come to believe about cultural relativity, ethnic or social diversity—nothing of that challenges what Kant and the whole project of the European Enlightenment was reaching for: the establishment, protection and enhancement of human freedom.

For Kant, the capacity for *thought,* for understanding, defines itself as one of the two central pillars of human-ness pure and simple, of freedom pure and simple. Call it, if you prefer, *consciousness*—that is, the laws and forms by which consciousness becomes aware of itself and the world. Consciousness in its garment of thought—deep thought, the deep, unfathomable movement toward, and yearning for, Understanding. Whether this force moves in the deep mind of an aboriginal tribesman or an

Asiatic shepherd or an Inuit hunter—whether it employs the abstract language of science or the symbolism of myth, dance or song—human consciousness ever moves in and from primal freedom and ever must obey the same self-discovered higher laws.

Kant and the noblest minds of the Enlightenment held firmly to this meaning surrounding the word "Reason," combining it with the second pillar of the human essence: the power of *will*. It is not Kant's fault that the social and cultural conditions within which Reason has expressed itself over the ages have sometimes—and especially in our time—led to the widespread denial of the meaning of Reason by emphasizing only the culturally varying adaptations of human thought to historical and environmental influences. Certainly it is true that just as individual human beings themselves are outwardly and psychologically conditioned by a vast spectrum of external influences of education and social expediency, forces which often produce a personality that overlays the universal human essence, so historically and culturally, whole civilizations have their own varying "personality." Yet we need to understand that behind and underneath such individual and cultural surfaces there continue to exist the universally human capacities and potentialities of Reason and will—or, as it might also be said, consciousness and conscience.

Nor is it Kant's fault that he did not explicitly treat the immense scale of possibility in the development of human consciousness. Nowhere in *The Critique of Pure Reason* does he seem to be aware of the levels of consciousness and the powers of action that are spoken of and fostered in the genuinely mystical or esoteric teachings of the world. But from that point of view, as we shall see, Kant should be viewed as a prophet of a future revolution rather than as a defender of sterile intellectualism. The Age of the Enlightenment begins and ends as a yearning to free the heart and mind and body of man—intellectually, morally, sexually and politically. Perhaps the power of real spirituality that, to some degree, is entering our world now can be seen as the next great step in that revolution, fulfilling it in ways that were called for by many of the great visionaries of the Enlightenment, such as Blake, Mozart, and Rousseau. Let the stringent "traditionalist" bemoan the modern loss of spiritual metaphysics. But let others of us see the modern era as a rebellion against the mind and body in chains, a rebellion that knew the goodness of freedom from slavery of all kinds, but which perhaps did not see deeply enough what freedom is for. Modernity: the realization of freedom *from*. The necessary new era: the call of what freedom is *for*.

I felt that I knew where Kant was going. He had to preserve science, he had to preserve Truth and Knowledge. And he had also to join Hume, even go one better than Hume, in chasing the dreamers and charlatans out of the temple of the mind. He had to cast out the demons of metaphysical fantasy and blind belief and make space for the true God of Knowledge.

Reading the pages of the *Critique* that followed, I immediately grasped Kant's great and simple idea. It is Reason itself that silently and invisibly organizes the fundamental structure of our experience of the world. And Reason *can with certainty* know *itself*. Reason can know its own fundamental principles with absolute certainty. What we can know with certainty are not the actual things and processes of the physical and biological world; no, what we can know with certainty are the overall, fundamental forms by which experience must be structured even as we receive it. The quarrel between the rationalists and the empiricists, the contradiction between their positions dissolves. Or, rather, each position finds its own true place—a sure sign that a higher reconciliation has been achieved. The true reconciling force never destroys; it always preserves and rescues the truth of both previous "adversaries."

Knowledge demands that we receive impressions of the external world through our senses. Knowledge of the world cannot be had just by sitting in one's chair and thinking. Therefore, the empiricists are right. Hume is right!

And yet human experience itself is unimaginable without formal, universal categories of Reason, such as the law of causality. Such categories are not truths about the world as it is in itself; that world can never be known by us. Yes, here, too, the empiricists are right. We have no direct experience of the things in themselves. But Kant goes even further than Hume. Not only, says Kant, do human beings have no direct experience of things in themselves; but they *cannot* have such experience. We do not

168

have minds that can penetrate directly into the reality that lies behind the screen of the formal laws and structures of our Reason.

But those formal structures are necessarily implied by the world that we do in fact experience! To know something, anything—plant, animal, Sun, Moon, water, stone—is to have already formed its fundamental nature, its fundamental being by means of the agency of human reason. Without these organizing principles there could be no experience! It would be in its way the equivalent of a logical contradiction. The law of contradiction—and other such laws and categories that Kant will describe—is necessarily true about the world—because it is necessarily true as the precondition of human experience. And this we can know *a priori*. It is certain knowledge about the world that we observe empirically—because it is knowledge of the laws of Reason by which mind irresistibly and invisibly shapes the form of the world that it perceives with the senses.

"Our nature is so constituted," writes Kant, "that . . . thoughts without [sensory] content are empty, [and] intuitions [sense perceptions] without concepts are blind."

My whole being relaxed and rejoiced. What he was bringing was an immense reconciling third force into the dualistic conflict between the mind and the senses, between reason and experience, between the rationalists and the empiricists.

As though rushing down upon me from my own mythic future was the intuition, without words, that everything that enthralled me about the stars and the life of living beings and ideas about man and God and the soul; everything that called me away from the dull and disillusioning world—everything that called to me from something like a higher world—all of that was at root the power of Truth as a reconciling force, the reconciliation of Mind in nature, in my life, in the world. All great insights, all visions of man and universe, all magic that called me away from my little egoism and dreams—it was all the power of some force that could bring together oppositions and conflicts into a greater whole, a mysterious, incomprehensible event prosaically labeled "the coincidence of opposites." It was in the mysterious smile of the Mona Lisa and all truly great art, it was in the eyes of the praying mantis, it was in the eyes of the beloved or in the face of the enemy suddenly perceived as a human being.

I was called by Knowledge and Knowledge was Life and Life was my God. Where Life was, there I would go.

CHAPTER TWELVE

The Cave of Absence

And, yes, *The Critique of Pure Reason* was more, far more even than a work of philosophical genius. Yes, the human mind, Reason, is driven, *called,* by its very nature to ask questions that it can neither answer nor ignore. Kant's genius was to build a vast cathedral of ideas on the altar of which he placed *proof*—proof that the mind, the intellect alone, can never know reality, can never know God. Proof that the great knowledge of science, though it can master the world in ways undreamt of before our modern era, yet at the same time, all this knowledge, all of our physics and biology and psychology, and all of our perceptions, bring us nothing more than *appearances.*

A despairing truth? Tales exist of extreme despair felt by many seekers of truth who came before this altar. But to me it brought joy. And its impact entered somewhere deeply into my nervous system and surfaced only many years later. Only now do I understand why, and why I feel a sense of great gratitude for the skepticism it unconsciously implanted and sustained in the back of my mind. And, even more deeply, for the unnameable hope it secretly emanated.

Down there, back there, in the depths or distance of my mind, Kant quietly slept while I conducted my life of the mind, freely studying and writing about existentialism, Eastern religion, Jewish and Christian mysticism, Plato, Socrates, Meister Eckhart, the teachings of Tibet and Zen Buddhism, the Bhagavad Gita and much else. All the while, Kant slept inside me. A place, a cave existed inside me, somewhere near the heart of the mind. In that place there existed—I could say, there *breathed*— not anything as simple or simplistic as atheism, or anything as positive as faith—it was something, someone, someone with my name, that I would now simply call the absence of conviction, the absence of real certainty—not the "certainty" that kills and blinds men, but the certainty that opens the heart and transforms the mind and rejoices the invisible body.

This absence is not recognized by our modern world; perhaps it has not been broadly recognized in any era of human history; and perhaps all the great truth that has been brought to the world has ultimately been meant to enter into that place, to fill that absence. I am speaking about the genuine truths brought to mankind by "those who knew," teachings that are meant to lead to the unlocking of that place of absence, bringing experience, direct experience of a kind unknown on the surface of the mind and the world, experience unimagined even in what is now conventionally called the unconscious or subconscious. Human culture, famous mystical writings, philosophers, scientists, artists, theologians, priests—it is all the same. Words are

used: empiricism, rationality, mystical states, higher consciousness, faith, free will, etc. In and around these words the intellectual and artistic and scientific life of mankind revolves, as it
revolved in my own growing life. And yet that place, that place
of absence, remained untouched, unknown, unrevealed—the
place of absence, the absence of certainty, the absence of conviction, the absence of being, the longing for truth—no matter
what that truth said. Only Truth can unlock that subterranean
door, no matter what that Truth says. Even if the Truth is that
there is no truth—the true conviction and certainty of even that
Truth is infinitely stronger than its content. Real Truth can never
bring despair because the real experience of Truth transforms
the knower into everything he had yearned for in vain from
words, from wise men, from worldly love, from virtue, adven-
ture, children, even "religion."

Who sleeps in that cave of absence where the yearning heart
of man and God waits to enter our actual life? Many legends tell
us we must find our way there through the strength of our desire for truth and the ability to love. But I think such legends are
wrong, or at least wrongly interpreted. We cannot find our
way there; we can only search on the surface of our lives, a surface that sometimes goes down very far, while yet remaining
surface—until that hidden door opens somehow from inside and
shows us at least a glimpse of what we have been longing for.
As I now see it, all talk of God, for or against, when it is honest,
is nothing more or less than so many prayers. We who pray in

this way, in this sense, can have no idea of what it will be like to have such prayers answered by a level or quality of experience we could not possibly have imagined.

At least so it has been in my case. And why this door opened, when I was young, bearing the name of Kant I cannot really say—unless it was the deeply hidden inner feeling of uncertainty, insecurity about all religious teaching, all philosophical claims, all moral doctrines, all literature and even all science, except what I actually saw with raw intensity with my own blazing eyes and held in my own flesh-and-blood hands—in my father's garden and in the star-strewn sky and in the thunder and lightning of death and violent grief. Down there, when I was younger, only Kant had somehow entered with his teaching about the mind's implacable striving to ask questions for which it can never find answers.

Part Three

CHAPTER THIRTEEN

The Atheist

August 2004

More than fifty years have passed since that September morning on the steps of Widener Library. During those years I have seen myself in thousands of students asking not just their professor, but the universe itself, questions that the mind alone cannot answer. From the very beginning I welcomed such questions, at first mainly out of professional duty to the calling of philosophy— philosophy as the vocation of thinking together about the questions of the heart. But gradually I not only welcomed but provoked such questions, because it became more and more clear that when such questions were sincerely asked, it was not possible to respond without trying to speak not only from my professional expertise, but from a deeper part of my own mind.

I did not often succeed. But the effort helped me to discover what I really owed my students, what I owed them of myself. And to discover how an entirely new understanding is given when one's sole motivation is to help another to understand.

There are hundreds of stories I could tell that deal with the idea and the question of God as it arose again and again in my classroom.

Here are two.

Her name was Verna, Verna Thatcher. She was now almost ninety years old—a short, plump lady with a few missing teeth, straggling gray hair and surprising youthful energy in her soft gray eyes and her soft, aging body. When she first started coming to my classes, she could still walk with the aid of a metal walker, but now she came in a wheelchair. Each semester there she was, always, planted in the center of the first or second row.

But why was she there?

"I don't understand what you're talking about," she would say, "when you talk about God. Where's the evidence?"

Speaking like that, she would look at me with suddenly fierce, firm eyes. Whether the text was Plato or Meister Eckhart, or the Bhagavad Gita or Emerson, sooner or later, when the word "God" was mentioned, there always appeared that steely look in the center of that open-hearted face. Five years had to pass before I discovered how to respond to that question and that look.

It was late in the summer, long after the academic year had ended. Months before, on the last day of the semester, I had asked if some people in the class would like to meet together informally. No required assignments, no examinations, no term papers, no grades. The aim would be to see if the kind of philo-sophical questions we had been studying could throw real light on how we actually lived our everyday lives and on how the threatened world actually works. About twenty students enthu-siastically put their names down on a piece of paper. Three months later I sent out an invitation. Five of them came—plus my young assistant.

The scene was a conference room lined with philosophy books. When your eyes wandered from the table, you were look-ing at *The Critique of Pure Reason. Beyond Good and Evil. Process and Reality. Language, Truth and Logic.* Or perhaps *The Quest for Certainty. On Liberty. Plato on Love. Why I Am Not a Christian. A Theory of Justice.* Titles, words that you might feel were seeing you even more than you were seeing them; as though one were surrounded by the mind's version of ancestor portraits looking down in distant judgment on their heirs and successors as they struggled to care for their lives with all that had been handed down to them. All the ideas, all the explanations, yes, but mainly: all the questions: What is Man? Why is there evil? What can we hope for? How should we live? And, above all perhaps, the ques-tion of God: Are we alone in the universe?

Was it not our first responsibility to care for these questions?

"I don't understand what you're talking about when you talk about God. Where's the evidence?" We had all only just sat down together around a conference table meant for many more than six or seven people. I had barely begun to open the dis-cussion when Verna coughed out these words, or something very like them. It was as though she had been carrying this question, this challenge, in the front of her mind all summer, just waiting for the moment when she could put it to me for the hundredth time.

This time I said nothing. To be honest, I did not really know what to say, how to respond. In that moment I felt more or less helpless. It seemed that in the years that she had been coming to my classes, I had used up every possible response, including ideas from some of history's greatest masters, and nothing had made a difference. It was not that I was trying, really, to convince her of anything. Well, maybe a little. But what most puzzled me and greatly interested me was that the question itself, "What is God? Does God exist?" never seemed to enter her, never seemed to be taken seriously. Yet Verna was no hardened academician with a profesional axe to grind; nor was she some fashionable author bent on selling atheism to the public. She was just a nice old lady who happened to believe there was no such thing as God. Wasn't she? Then why was she untouched by the universal power of this question?

And why, then, had she been coming to my classes every semester for five years? It could not have been easy for her to get there—and now she even had to engage a caregiver to accompany her and help her with her physical needs. She could not walk, she could hardly hear, even with a complex hearing apparatus hanging around her neck. "I have never experienced anything like what you're speaking about," she would say, defiantly.

And why did I think of her, finally, as the most serious

person in my class? More than that. I thought of her as one of the most *spiritually* serious of all my students.

And that, too, only became clearer to me on that particular day, after five years.

I had begun to imagine what she might have been like as a young woman. I pictured the young Verna attending countless talks and living-room meetings on social causes, marching to support labor and equal rights for women, poring over the writings of philosophers and economists, bent on exposing the tyranny of capitalism and religious dogma, surrounded by and immersed in what seemed in those days the freedom of the mind to think for oneself and, with the advances of science, to bring humanity into a new era of justice and community. Those were the days in which scientific method was implicitly understood, not simply as an abstract system of investigative procedures, but as what John Dewey had identified as a social practice, a concrete realization of the true ideal of democracy. Applying the words of one observer, it was "the openness of scientific inquiry, the imagination required for its successful practice, the willingness to submit hypotheses to public test and criticism, the intrinsic communal and cooperative character of scientific community"[48]—it was this that made of modern science a powerful moral and, in its own way, spiritual ideal for many of the best minds and purest hearts of an entire generation of Americans.

I all but started picturing how she looked and dressed when she was young.

In any case, so I imagined, it was for Verna as it had been

for many of us a badge of honor to believe in science and in the awakening power of humanity to take responsibility for oneself and for the human world, and to free oneself from what Freud had so persuasively identified as the *illusion* of religion.[49]

A thick silence was enveloping everyone. Through the large windows behind my back the sun was lowering and filling the room with a darkening gold light. Two unshaven undergraduate men sat like illuminated stones at the far end of the conference table. On my right, directly across the table from Verna, was one of my graduate students who almost always had something to say, but he too only fidgeted a little without uttering a word. To my immediate right was my young assistant, still and silent. Everyone was waiting for me to reply. But I didn't and couldn't. There was some kind of tiredness in me, not physical, but, in a way, moral. I was not trying some kind of Zen-like maneuver. I could not even say I was waiting, silently, for her or someone else to speak. I felt no anxiety whatever about just sitting there without a word. I wouldn't have minded at all if everyone had just gotten up and walked out. I was tired not only of trying to answer questions, but even of the simple human obligation of responding. I felt that I could have stayed like that for an hour, maybe even forever. I was tired of the obligation to try to help people think. Out of the corner of my mind (or somewhere) I understood that although I was quite alert, I felt no desires at all, of any kind, physical, emotional, or mental.

My fidgeting graduate student did finally try to help what he must have felt was a difficult situation by questioning Verna about her definition of the word "evidence," or some such textbook maneuver. But the silence swallowed his words like a whale swallowing a small fish. If anything, his words served only to heighten the intensity of the silence.

Looking back on this event, I suppose it had been given to me to have entered perhaps the outskirts of what the ancient teachings call a "desireless state." The steady alertness I felt was unlike anything I had ever experienced in my life as a teacher. It was a bright, calm attention with no "wiring" connecting it to any impulse to do or manifest anything. No impulse to explain or help. No craving to protect my self-image. Or to "shoulder my responsibility." It was an attention that flowed through my mind, heart and body without mingling at all with the interests, passions and impulses emanating from these three fundamental parts of my human nature.

I don't know how much time passed until finally I said something to Verna. "There may be some things that can't be understood by the mind alone," I said. "There are different kinds of knowing. It may be that past a certain point the question of God cannot be approached with the mind alone. By itself, mental knowing may be intrinsically incapable of recognizing what God really is."

Verna's guard immediately went down. "What do you mean?" she said hastily.

"What I mean is that the human mind, the whole of the

human psyche, may be much, much more vast and complex than we imagine, with many more sources of perception than we can imagine."

I was more or less ready to stop right there. But for some reason I went on, without feeling any real need to convince her of anything. Looking back on the event, I now see what it was that somehow lent a certain authority, believability, to what was said. It was my state, unusual for me in my role as a professor: my state of "disinterest."

But let me try to be clearer about what I am calling "disinterest." It was not indifference. Far from it. But somehow, because I had given up all hope of trying to "win her over," "awaken her mind," make her understand—because all that kind of motivation had fallen away—something entirely new had appeared in my attitude toward her and toward the question we were facing. Somehow, because I had happened to have given all that up in this special, specific relationship with this special, specific person, a strange and strangely quiet kind of *faith* had appeared in me.

But faith in what?

"There's a knowledge in the mind," I said, "but there's also a knowledge in the heart and in the body. And for all the important questions of life, these three sources of knowledge have to come together."

I paused.

And then I continued. "When you love someone or something you can understand things about them that you cannot understand or even perceive with the mind alone. Isn't that so?

When you look up at a sky full of stars you understand something about the universe that no purely mental process can fathom.

"And there is knowledge in the body also. When you learn to play a musical instrument or ride a bicycle or draw a picture or throw a pot, it's essential that the body learns and knows, don't you think?

"And human beings are gifted with the possibility, and maybe the necessity, the duty of bringing all these sources of knowing together. That's what reason really is. Everything else that is called by that name can be done also by a computer or an animal. It may be that the question of God can really be approached only with all three sources of knowing working together . . ."

As I continued in this vein, I became more and more interested in my own state of even, untroubled self-attention. It is true that I spoke without any impulse to persuade or convince her, or even to help her. But that would not be the whole truth. The whole truth is much more interesting than that. I see now, looking back on the event, that I was somehow speaking to a completely different part of her, a part of the human being that I had perhaps never addressed in my work as a professional teacher of philosophy. I was speaking to Verna behind Verna— and I did not even really know it at the time. I did not have to persuade *Verna-behind-Verna*. All that was needed was that I speak, or *be*, in a way that allowed Verna-behind-Verna to appear.

But also—and this is, if anything, of even greater

importance—it was not Professor Jacob Needleman who happened to be speaking. This I see now very clearly. It was, to a degree, *I-behind-me* who had arrived in the room.

Ralph Waldo Emerson speaks of how "Jove nods to Jove in each one of us." So it was here. Verna's eyes widened. Her face became still, quiet, intensely, dynamically alive. Her old body began to straighten. She looked at me—through me—with a look of a kind that I had seen countless times in my young students, but in her, in this woman of many years, that same look went deep, deep into herself—or should I say came from deep, deep in her self, breaking through who knows how many years and decades of imprisonment, and therefore all the more powerful and penetrating than in the face of a younger person. It was not just the look of an awakening mind—that is wonderful enough, and when it appears it is what makes the teaching of philosophy worth everything. Yes, it was that, but also something more.

Entirely more.

CHAPTER FOURTEEN

The Fundamentalist

I was immediately drawn to this man, Brennan O'Brien; his amazing orange-red hair and his delicious Irish brogue—"Well now, Professor, and how be *you* this fine day?"

I guessed him to be in his early thirties, craggy features, pale eyes, high forehead plowed with wrinkles. Black Bible under his arm, he took his seat every day in the geometric center of the class. Then he carefully placed his Bible squarely on the swing-out writing surface of his chair.

I immediately labeled him "fundamentalist." And I prepared my mind accordingly. Over the years I have had many students to whom this label applies. At first, when I was starting out as a teacher, they unnerved me with their icy literalism about scripture and their often hostile certainty that only surrender to *their* Jesus Christ could lead to salvation. I never really tried to reason with them or understand them. But neither did I deny them their right to speak. I only tried to move on and not get tangled in my reactions.

I did not always succeed. I often got annoyed, angry. Didn't they know what kind of course this was? It was philosophy—the attempt to think independently about the fundamental questions of human life. Good and evil. Life. Death. Suffering. Justice. Knowledge and illusion. And one of those fundamental questions—or, perhaps, all of these questions together—was the question of God. Didn't they know, weren't they aware, that our work was to step back in ourselves and separate ourselves from our assumptions and our beliefs in order to think like grown-ups? In order to free ourselves, if only a little and for only an hour or so, from the tendency of the mind to become the slave of the emotions? In any case, they must surely have read the course description in the catalog, where it was clear that we would be examining—critically, but sympathetically—the teachings of several religions and philosophies and not just *their* Christianity.

Over the years I came to realize how naïve I had been about this. I began to see that the willingness and the ability to separate from one's own thoughts, opinions and assumptions was not as common a property as I had imagined. But, even so, I continued to believe that this act of the mind—to step back from itself—could be cultivated in almost anyone. And I had imagined that my obligation as a teacher of philosophy was to help students to discover this power of the mind which for many of us is the first step toward deep inner freedom and genuine faith. It was the centrality of this power of the mind that Socrates brought to the Western world through his famous and often misinterpreted statement about his own "ignorance."

As almost every college freshman learns, there was in ancient Greece a temple at Delphi in which a visionary woman responded to questions with oracular pronouncements of uncommon wisdom and prescience. Known as the Oracle of Delphi, she was once asked who was the wisest man in Athens—so the story goes. She answered that the wisest man in Athens was Socrates. Through Plato's telling of the story, we learn that Socrates at first refused to believe the Oracle since he had long since realized that he himself really understood nothing at all. And so, to prove the Oracle wrong, he went around Athens inquiring among those whose actions or creative work led them to believe in their own understanding and gave them the reputation or the appearance of wisdom. But after questioning statesmen, scientists, poets, artists, craftsmen and others who claimed or seemed to have wisdom of one sort or another, he discovered that they too understood nothing of any real significance. He discovered that the Oracle was right—he was indeed the wisest man, but only because he alone was aware of his ignorance.

This story is the elephant in the living room of the whole enterprise of philosophy, the whole ideal of independent thought in the Western world. Reading about Socrates, anyone with any sense at all realizes that he understood very much indeed and about many things—about the soul, about good and evil, about love, friendship, honor, beauty, nature—many things. Then why does he claim ignorance? Is it only irony, meant to provoke self-questioning in the other? Yes, perhaps, partly. But if that were all it was, it would have been seen through after one or two such gestures, and it would have soon lost its effectiveness. Was it that he had such a high standard of what it means to understand that he honestly realized his own level of knowledge fell far short of true wisdom? That comes closer to the mark, but it does not go far enough. The ignorance of Socrates is a much more dynamic thing. It has the power of irresistible action in the midst of dialogue, in the midst of human relationship—in the midst of the most important form of human relationship (that is to say, love): the shared search for truth, the shared search for truth that one experiences for oneself and in oneself—not someone else's truth, not even God's truth (unless we understand God in a thunderously new way); my own truth discovered by my very own mind here and now, within myself; truth that therefore has the power to transform my life, my acts, my very being.

No, Socratic ignorance is invisible to us because we try to clothe it with something we can understand and explain. We step around this elephant while throwing garments over it. But when the elephant moves, it terrifies us. Socratic ignorance represents in fact the power of the empty, silent mind, the mind free of preoccupation with ideas and thoughts, the mind purified. And in and from this purified mind there arises a new quality of mind: call it pure attention.

I see now that this possibility of pure attention is something that I glimpsed very, very dimly when I was first drawn to the study of philosophy. Even as a young teenager studying philosophical texts that I could in no way fully grasp, there arose the fleeting taste of the independent mind. As the powerful writings of the great philosophers forced me to become aware of my assumptions and beliefs, sitting in the safety of my small bedroom or alone at twilight parked behind the wheel of the family car, I would sometimes be given a moment of emptiness and inner silence. Ideas were being offered to me that were so big that they silenced all my opinions and all my own little ideas which had over time crawled into my mind and made their nests there.

Over the years I had developed the ability to recognize which students, which people had what I was calling a "philosophical temper." I became able to see, sometimes instantly, in which people there was a wish, an inclination, an ability to step back in oneself and begin to ponder, to wish to follow truth wherever it might lead. This quality, this philosophical temper, is not at all the same thing as academic ability or skill in this or that area of knowledge—science, literature, languages, etc. It can exist in anyone—in a poet, in a craftsman, in a waiter, in a businessman, even in a child. And where it does *not* exist is as surprising as where it does exist. So many eminent scholars, scientists, professional philosophers were lacking in this quality, often covering it over with the mere belief that they possessed it—so I found. Yes, this ideal was the great ideal of the Age of Enlightenment in the Western world. Nevertheless, to profess the ideal and actually to live it are very different things—so I found.

And here was this Brennan O'Brien with his flaming hair

and pale eyes. Why did I immediately feel so interested in him? The questions he asked and the observations he made showed he was every inch the "fundamentalist" I took him to be. Where, for example, our text would speak of symbolic meanings in the Bible, he would simply accuse the author of arrogance. Where comparisons of elements in different spiritual teachings were introduced, such as the Buddhist ideal of non-attachment together with the Stoic idea of *ataraxia* and the early Christian doctrine of *apatheia*—all of which involve inner freedom from being overpowered by personal emotions—here my Mr. O'Brien would have none of it, to the point even of denying that there was a profound inner, psychospiritual dimension in the Christian teaching. And as for the evidence offered in the writings of the great Christian contemplatives—those masters of the inner life, the early Fathers in the deserts of North Africa—or the sermons of Meister Eckhart, the writings of Hildegard or Teresa of Ávila—here, with clenched jaw, Mr. O'Brien simply sat still as a stone with his arms rigidly crossed over his heart as though protecting it from danger.

But, if I may put it this way, his "emanations" gave the lie to his grim expression and his stiff posture. His pale eyes glowed with attention.

The generic name of the course was "Modern Religious Thought." Such courses are taught in very different ways by different professors, each selecting the books they wish to use; and whoever teaches it is free to emphasize any aspect of this broad area that he or she considers important. And each professor is invited to attach a descriptive title to the course, indicating its main emphasis for that particular semester.

The descriptive title I had given was "The Metaphysical Critique of Modernity." The aim was to look at the threatened world we now live in from a point of view that has its source far, far back in time—a great underground stream of ideas and practice that repeatedly rises to the surface of human history. And which softly, repeatedly—in differing languages and forms—sounds its call to humanity: "Stop!" "Learn to look at yourselves!" "Learn to remember the high Reality in yourselves that you ignore, and recognize the falsehood in yourselves that you believe in."

As the basis of the course, I assigned two powerful books by authors who have not yet found their way into the established academic curriculum: *The Crisis of the Modern World*[50] by René Guénon and *A New Model of the Universe*[51] by P. D. Ouspensky. Early in the twentieth century, when, even after World War I, the modern world still believed in itself, each of these men, following his own unique intuition, and writing with a sometimes unnerving tone of authority, articulated a profound response to the great "questions of the heart." At the same time, the writings of each cast a nearly blinding light on the main components of modern, Western culture: from its noble ideals of scientific truth to its destructively naïve scientism and technocentrism; from its longing for human rights and shared material well-being to its heedless economic and nationalistic ideologies, its monstrous fascism, its dreamy and murderous communism and its hypocritical, rampant capitalism; from its high educational goal of freeing the mind to its abandonment and profanation of the spirit of transcendence in the rising generation; from its respect for fact and the laws of nature to its brutalization of nature and the earth; and, finally, from its unsung, poignant refusal to abandon its longing for God to its helpless alternation of exploitation, manipulation, and embalming of the symbols, rituals and doctrines of religion.

It was midway through the course, when we were reading Ouspensky's chapter on Christianity and the New Testament, that I clearly understood what it was about Mr. O'Brien that had so touched me from the very first day.

Until now he had listened with rigid posture to the merciless critique of modernity by Guénon, a critique based on Guénon's vision of an ancient primordial tradition from which all civilizations and great religions, including Christianity, had arisen. To a fundamentalist, of course, such a theory about the origins of religion is repugnant, situating Christianity as no more (but also no less) than one among many of mankind's authentic sacred traditions. Nevertheless, Mr. O'Brien had restrained himself and voiced his questions and objections without insisting on them.

But Ouspensky's view of Christianity was another matter, and here Mr. O'Brien's cup of restraint overflowed. Nor was this surprising. One did not have to be a fundamentalist to balk at what Ouspensky speaks of as the "esoteric" meaning of the Gospels and the esoteric core of Christianity itself. According to Ouspensky, the Christian religion as we know it, and as it has spread throughout the world and throughout the history of the world, is in very large measure a distortion of the teaching of Christ and the principles of the community that was intentionally formed around him.

The chief thing that has been generally forgotten, according to Ouspensky, is the precise inner work of cultivating self-knowledge, without which the scriptures, doctrines, symbols and rituals of Christianity lose their essential function as instruments in a process, the end result of which is the transformation of human nature: *the new man*. Unlike Guénon, who speaks only in general terms of higher levels of "the being" in man, Ouspensky's book is strewn with experientially verifiable indications concerning the mental, moral, and even bodily characteristics of this "new man" that is our fundamental human possibility.

In any case, on every page of both books are ideas which pose a spectacular challenge, not just to fundamentalists, but to almost anyone at all, be he religious, humanist, atheist or something else. The arguments of these two writers are as difficult to dismiss as they are hard to swallow.

We Begin to Think

Mr. O'Brien calmly raised his hand.

He began by referring to something we had spoken about earlier in the semester: the fact that the word "Christianity" can mean many different things, depending on whether one is Catholic or Protestant or Orthodox, or any one of the numerous branches within or outside of these denominations.

His voice was strong without being loud; even, yet crackling with feeling.

"I think the problem is what you were discussing at the beginning of the class," he said, "about how there are so many so-called Christianities today."

He paused.

"And therein lies the problem."

He went on:

"The Word of God itself says that God is not *the author of confusion*. And the Apostle Peter himself tells us that no prophecy of Scripture is of any private interpretation.[52] So . . . for you to take your interpretation of the Bible, and for me to take my interpretation of the Bible—he is saying that's the wrong way to go."

He paused again.

"So where *do* we go?" I asked.

"We go to the Bible," he said.

Laughter in the class. One rarely encounters such a blatant example of circular reasoning in an advanced philosophy class.

I did not laugh. Whatever else Mr. O'Brien was, he was not a fool.

Unfazed by the laughter, Mr. O'Brien continued:

"If you go to the Book of Isaiah," he said, in the same strong, even voice, "the prophet speaks about how shall we teach knowledge and whom shall we make understand doctrine or teaching. And speaking through the prophet, God says, 'for precept must be upon precept, line upon line, here a little and there a little.'[53] In other words, you don't just try to take one little passage in Scripture and try to understand what it's saying based upon your own feelings and your own emotions. No, you take that one passage and find another place in the Bible where the same idea is being talked about, and you establish the meaning. . . ."

I did not happen to be familiar with the context of that passage in Isaiah. I did suspect that Mr. O'Brien was, ironically enough, offering only one among many possible interpretations of it. But that hardly mattered at the moment. What mattered was that something was beginning to pass between him and me, between his mind and my mind. For me, it was the first time I was actually trying to listen, to let the mind of a "fundamentalist" into myself. To allow it to enter into me.

He continued:

". . . because the Bible says that there is one Lord, one faith, and one baptism. So—there is only one faith that the Bible is speaking of, but all of a sudden, today, we have everybody saying a different thing. Everybody has a different teaching, everybody has a different faith. The Catholics, the Protestants, the Baptists, everybody is saying a different thing. But the Bible is very strict about saying there is one faith . . ."

My feelings were understanding this man quite well. I saw that I had very different ideas, but at the same time I glimpsed something else, something important, something new. I saw that he and I had the same—or a very similar—kind of feeling about truth, but very different ideas about the mental content of truth. But I didn't want to think more about this, even though it suddenly seemed to be the key to something of momentous importance in the way mankind divides itself, in the way mankind suffers from the delusion of difference, when underneath the head, as it were, there may be entirely unknown forces of relationship. But I tried to push these intimations aside. In order to keep letting Mr. O'Brien in.

". . . so the way that you find that one faith is not by taking someone's interpretation. Mine or yours or someone else's. You need to let the Bible interpret itself."

Mr. O'Brien continued. But now my mind was flooded with responses to what he had just said, *You need to let the Bible interpret itself*. As he was explaining what he meant by that, I found myself, paradoxically, both fully open to hear his thought *and* fully open to my own mind at the same time. Lights were going on in me. But far from distracting me from him, these "lights" seemed to be opening me more and more to him and also to the whole class. This process in myself, I soon realized, was a process of a new kind of thinking, not under the sway of passing time, not one thought after another, not logic, not imaging, but something else. But whatever it was, it was *thought*. I knew I had much now to bring to this question of letting the Bible interpret itself. Was this not the dream of many of the great philosophers of the Western world?—the dream of freeing oneself from hidden assumptions, from prejudices of every kind, from dogma: was this not the whole dream of the unfettered mind? How could this attitude ever have decayed into fundamentalist dogmatism— into the very specter of tyranny over the mind of man? But more than that. What of this feeling that I was more and more deeply sharing with Mr. O'Brien? Did he sense that, too? Did the class— all these student eyes wide open, bodies unmoving, lips parted— did they sense something unique taking place between the professor and the student?

At this point I wanted to say something to the class, to include them in what was happening between me and Mr. O'Brien. I wanted to call attention to the overt emotional aspect of the question of interpreting the Bible. And I wanted to prepare the class for what I now saw was possible and necessary, namely, the question of the influence of emotion on thought: both the egoistic emotions that are mostly what we live by, and which ultimately are the source of division and violence, and the subtler currents of deeper, organic feeling that go largely unnoticed and which have the power to connect us to each other.

And if it is a new kind of feeling, harmonized with the vibration, and not necessarily the intellectual content, of thought, that can truly connect human beings with each other, how could a connection with whatever we call God be possible with less than that? Does not God, whatever He, She, or It is, also feel? If God is love, as it is said, is not God's love also a feeling? Such questions, although chaotic in form, were now burning in me. I wanted somehow, some way, to pursue them with the class. I wanted to share such a question with these young men and women. I knew from experience that a deeper form of learning takes place when the teacher shares a real question with his or her students. Under the wing of a shared genuine (not artificial) question, all concepts, facts and academic comparisons suddenly take root in the mind and become meaningful and alive.

But Mr. O'Brien wanted to say more:

"Okay, say the Bible is talking about repentance. You read it, and instead of saying 'This is what it means,' you look elsewhere in the book where it's talking about repentance. Okay, let's find somewhere else where Jesus or the Apostle Paul, or someone else is talking about repentance. And let's see if what I thought that meant lines up with what this other scripture is saying . . ."

Hardly revolutionary; few serious readers of the Bible or any text would disagree—except that what Mr. O'Brien was saying was that one need not, and perhaps should not, turn to any other interpretation at all. That is the whole dramatic point of his scriptural fundamentalism.

And it is not as foolish as it appears. Or is it?

Is it not the way a genuine scientist looks at nature? A genuine poet looks at nature, at life? A great artist, a great writer and thinker? How to stand on the shoulders of giants and, as it were, stand on one's own feet at the same time? How to see directly and yet be served by the great minds of the past? What a question! What a question to suddenly feel in the midst of thinking together with another man or woman with whom one at first imagined there could be absolutely no connection! How did it happen that a fundamentalist was suddenly channeling into the mind of the class the whole depth and breadth of the question of man's knowledge of God, nature, and one's own Self?

I realized that it was necessary to follow through to the end with Mr. O'Brien. But I was bursting with the wish to take the discussion toward the profound question of the relationship between emotion and how we understand what God is. We educate our minds about how to think—logically, rationally—and our thinking, as it is, leads some of us to science and some to religion; just as within ourselves, there often exist two separate people, one of whom is scientific and the other religious. But in all this, we do not educate our feeling; we do not even know what this would mean, really. Mentally we and our society are very advanced, *sort of*—but emotionally we remain as children. Well, it is obviously true, isn't it?

The class was coming to an end—students packing up their

computers and books and looking at their watches. Mercifully, I did not have to choose between staying with Mr. O'Brien, which I very much wished to do—and opening the question of the nature of emotion, which I was *yearning* to do.

I promised myself that I would take care of both needs in the next class—on Tuesday.

CHAPTER FIFTEEN

Tuesday

I had brought with me some passages from William James about religious emotion, by means of which I planned to open the question of the cognitive function of emotion—that is, the question of whether emotion of a specific kind brings us knowledge about certain essential issues that thought alone cannot bring us. My hidden agenda was to explore the possibility (which I believe to be a certainty) that the ordinary mind alone cannot know, or even know much about, what we may call God. To put it more bluntly, when left to itself our ordinary mind, by which we deduce, infer, calculate and theorize, is, so to say, consciously or not, a dyed-in-the-wool "atheist." But also: our ordinary, everyday emotional part alone, without a relationship to the mind, is a "fanatic." As for the necessary role of the physical body in the search for genuine knowledge, I recognized that I did not understand enough nor had I the right to try to bring anything but the theoretical aspect of this question into an academic setting.

But before reading the passages from William James to the class, I began by once again addressing Mr. O'Brien.

"Religion is a very passionate subject, isn't it?"

"I wouldn't call myself religious," said Mr. O'Brien, surprising everyone.

"Well, you are passionate about it."

"Well," he said, "I suppose you could say I'm passionate."

"In my opinion, this can be a very good thing—to have a strong feeling about whatever it is we call truth." I was a little uneasy about the way that came out of me. Suddenly, if only a little, I myself was in question.

"I believe in it, yes."

"I appreciate that," I said. "But don't we also need to be able to think critically?"

I didn't care for that either. My words were becoming shallow, professorial.

Mr. O'Brien did not reply immediately.

I continued: "What do you bring to Scripture?" I asked. He looked at me quizzically.

"It's the same question for a scientist, for anyone: What do I bring to nature, to anything? What is the instrument of knowing?"

Again, he said nothing.

"We bring *ourselves,* yes? You say, open the Bible and look at it."

"Yes."

"Who is opening it? Who is looking at it?"

"I was only saying that the Bible is a spiritual book."

"I'd say that, too," I answered.

He went on: "And in order to understand that book, you've got to have the spirit of the book in yourself. The spirit of God."

"And how does a person come to that? From where does it come?

Mr. O'Brien paused. I knew what he was about to say. And he said it.

"You get the spirit of God from God."

Again, laughter in the class—but much softer, much less sure of itself. I believe at that point the class was reflecting the change of tone that was taking place in the professor and the student. I was going to proceed as far as I felt necessary with the role of philosophical interrogation, but at the same time my sense of warmth toward Mr. O'Brien was increasing, strongly. And, for his part, his voice was not quite as clear and steady as before. I had the impression he was, for a moment, actually trying to step back in himself, trying to step back from his beliefs.

"Saint Paul talks about this," he said. "He says that the carnal mind is at enmity with God. He says that the carnal mind is not subject to the laws of God, neither can it be. He says that unless you have the spirit of God, you can't understand the things of God."

"And how do you get the spirit of God?" I asked, and I heard myself muting the sense of challenge in the question. I was beginning to understand, right then and there, the human-ness of Mr. O'Brien's religious emotion. In him this religious emotion was a little like being in love, I thought. His craggy face and cool eyes made him look strong and unshakable. But I couldn't help feeling that he was baring his heart and that his illogically "logical" mind had surrendered itself, perhaps enslaved itself, to something in his heart. And I wondered: What will happen to him if I keep pressing him with questions of Biblical interpretation that critically challenge the literal reading of scripture, a literalism that, in Mr. O'Brien's case was, as it seemed to me, completely in the service of his passionate religious emotion. Identified with such emotional thinking, a man or woman cannot and cannot even wish to *step back* in oneself. No more than a narrowly and purely logical mind can allow itself to move in the opposite direction and leave its separateness in order to allow the entering into itself of the passion of love or emotion. I was shocked to find myself taking the role—no, not just taking the role, but believing in it, being swallowed by it—the role of the logical academician, the intellect isolated from the heart. What did it matter if what I would say was echoing (or, rather, parroting) the profound mystical insights of masters of spiritual wisdom, or that Mr. O'Brien was saying things that reflected the mere surface readings of the ocean of Biblical teachings? I was shocked, as I went on, to realize that I was not right and he was not wrong. What was at stake was far more fundamental. I was a head and he was a heart, much as it may have seemed otherwise from the outside.

But something of even more fundamental importance was about to take place.

"And how do you get the spirit of God?" I had said.

He replied, "You get the spirit of God by repenting." He paused and looked at me, and then for a moment bowed his head. What was he doing? Was he thinking, considering? Was he realizing something about himself? All I could see was his flaming orange hair.

He raised his head and continued: "By renouncing the world and the things of this world."

I suddenly realized that Mr. O'Brien was utterly vulnerable. But so was I. I had started to speak, when several students called out that they couldn't hear me. I realized that I was speaking in a very soft voice—as though it was just myself and Mr. O'Brien alone. I was nearly whispering.

"But what does renunciation mean?" I said, trying to speak more loudly. The meaning of this word, this idea, this spiritual necessity, was opening in my mind, in my memory. "Renunciation—it doesn't only mean giving up external things, does it?"

"But," said Mr. O'Brien, his brow now wrinkled, "this is what Jesus was talking about! He went to a rich man. He said, you lack one thing; go sell everything that you have, and follow me."

"But," I answered, more and more feeling the sense of commitment behind Mr. O'Brien's words, "what is a rich man?"

For the first time, he looked around at the class, as though asking for their support. "Someone who has a lot of money." And then he skipped a beat, his eyes looking up for a thought: "So it's whatever is holding you back . . ."

"So, you see . . ." I started—

". . . from God, holding you back from God. Jesus says, let it go."

I started to say, "Whatever 'a rich man' means—it's something that's holding him back . . ."

Mr. O'Brien sharply interrupted me, his pale eyes strong and steady again. Maybe too strong, too steady.

"It's the *riches* that's holding him back. When Jesus says 'a rich man,' he means a rich man. He's not trying to use metaphors!" And he paused, and then something quite new came out of him: "I don't believe Jesus is using metaphors." What was new was the *I don't believe!*

I did not feel much inclination to argue the point. But I felt I owed him my own conviction—not to convince him, but only to stay in relationship with him—in the way a person often talks about anything at all to a friend just to stay in relationship.

At that point, however, I stopped. The class had become noticeably still and silent, observing whatever it was that was happening between myself and Mr. O'Brien. And just then I realized what was actually taking place. *A heart was moving toward the head; and a head was moving toward the heart.* And Mr. O'Brien and I were meeting somewhere in that middle, intermediate zone where an entirely new kind of feeling was beginning to appear: *a feeling that was like a thought, and a thought that was like a feeling.*

We were beginning to understand each other. Not in

words—he and I still disagreed—but in the sense that his and my *inner states* had begun to harmonize with each other. Alone, by itself, the head cannot understand the heart, nor can the heart accept the head. And metaphysically, it means little when two lopsided, isolated intellects either converge or diverge: the result is only to reinforce each other's lopsided state of being. And, in its more frequent and extreme form, it also means little (although it may have huge and often disastrous consequences in practice) when two emotional centers converge or diverge: the result is more often than not heat without light, the kind of passion that, when it meets its first great difficulty, can destroy the world.

I reached for William James.

CHAPTER SIXTEEN

God and the Emotions

I will try now to recapture on the printed page what was for me the extraordinary process of entering into a serious question, not with one student but with fifty students at the same time.

I had just finished reading to the class several passages from William James's *The Varieties of Religious Experience*.

This book is a uniquely fertile source of questions about the nature and value of religious life. James, a Harvard professor of philosophy and psychology, was invited over a hundred years ago to deliver the prestigious Gifford Lectures to an academic and scientifically oriented public in Edinburgh, Scotland. In these lectures James pioneered the psychological study of phenomena such as faith, the sense of sin, saintliness, conversion and mystical states of consciousness. And he did so without in any way regarding these phenomena of religious life as reducible to mechanistic, biological, or sociological elements, as was the habit of the academic/scientific community of his time (and of our time, as well). On the contrary, what gives this book its power is that James succeeds in blending scientific logic and spiritual sensitivity—that is to say, in bringing together his own mind and heart to the study of religious experience.

In what I read to the class, James was seeking to define his subject by noting the problem of treating what is called "the religious sentiment" (or emotion) as one single sort of psychological entity. On the contrary, says James, the religious sentiment can be allied to many different kinds of emotion—fear, for example, or sexual desire, or the feeling of the infinite. James concludes that religious feeling cannot be identified with any one specific emotion, but can ally itself with many different human emotions. "There is religious fear," he says, "religious awe, religious joy, and so forth." For example, religious love, he says,

> *is only man's natural emotion of love directed to a religious object; religious fear is only the ordinary fear of commerce, so to speak, the common quaking of the human breast, in so far as the notion of divine retribution may arouse it; religious awe is the same organic thrill which we feel in a forest at twilight, or in a mountain gorge; only this time it comes over us at the thought of our supernatural relations; and similarly of all the various sentiments [emotions] which may be called into play in the lives of religious persons.*[54]

When I had first read this passage many years ago, it had struck me as simple common sense. Fear is fear, love is love; only the objects differ—so James, the scientific psychologist, thought, and so it had then seemed to me. But I had now come to see things quite differently. Quite differently. I had come to the indubitable conclusion that there exists in man a stunning, qualitative difference in the very nature of authentic, spiritual emotion, a difference that the modern world has failed to recognize. It was this question that I wanted to open up in the class—because the idea of God can never be studied without at least a theoretical recognition and appreciation of this question of the nature of emotion.

And it is with James that such questions come to life as they do in few other works of philosophy. They come to life because of what has been called James's "pluralism"—that is, his ability to entertain and lucidly present multiple, even contradictory ideas about many of the most central aspects of his subject, and especially about the nature of religious emotion. For, not long after he has characterized religious emotion as ordinary emotion that just happens to have a religious object, he says of religious emotion that it is an entirely different kind of emotion, what he calls a "higher kind of emotion,"[55] having an entirely different kind and power of action within the self.

James leads this conversational presentation of what seem like contradictory points of view without provoking the least suspicion that it is a weakness in his thought. On the contrary, it is so artlessly and naturally done as to evoke in the reader a gentle invitation to follow the text by thinking for oneself. And it is that aspect of James's work—the invitation to think for oneself—that I hoped to share with the whole class.

So, rather than going forward with the text, I found myself asking the class to close their books and simply tell me how they felt today. It was an impulse on my part. I really did not have a clear idea of where I would go with it. I wanted to try, together with the class, to think for myself about this question of religious emotion. And to think for myself meant, for me as well as for the class, not knowing the answer in advance.

In that spirit, after a few minutes of uncomfortable silence, I changed the question slightly. But that change made all the difference. The class came alive.

"How do you feel *now*?" I said, and then, after another silence, this time not uncomfortable, but energized: "I mean *right now*, in this very moment."

A young man with a wispy beard smiled and answered: "Nervous."

On impulse, I wrote on the blackboard: *Nervous.*

Immediately, I knew where I was going; I knew absolutely what the next step had to be. The next step in opening the question. The next step in entering the unknown—in bringing myself and the whole class in front of a perhaps impossible, but necessary, question. I had no idea how or if the answer would appear. But I had faith that some form of answer or direction of thought would be given. The experience of this kind of faith is, for me, the most precious element in the work of teaching and writing and thinking with others.

With the word "nervous" at my back, I asked the class again: "How do you feel, right now?" I looked at Melissa Cramer, sitting off to the side. She stuttered for a moment and then said, "Overwhelmed."

I turned around and wrote *overwhelmed* underneath *nervous*. As I was writing, a male voice called out, "Hungry!" There was some good-natured laughter as I obediently wrote *hungry* on the board. But was "hungry" really an emotion? Or was it more accurately a sensation? I wrote it anyway, promising myself to bring the point up later. An important point.

I turned around to face the class. They once again seemed paralyzed. What was Professor Needleman doing? Strangely, I saw that it was not always so easy to say—or even to know— what one is feeling. I myself didn't know, couldn't name exactly what, if anything, I was feeling. Was my mind really such a fool? Here was another important point—wasn't it? How interesting, I thought. Realizing that I—like the class—did not know what I was feeling, could not name what I was feeling, I began to . . . feel? . . . sense? . . . become aware of a fine, quiet vibration passing through me.

On another impulse, but much calmer this time, I changed the question again. "All right," I said. "Name an emotion, any emotion." I became more recognizably "the professor" again, allowing a purely intellectual task to guide the inquiry. But what resulted at first was—predictably, no doubt—meager.

"Happiness," said one student. I wrote it on the blackboard.

"Fear," said another. I wrote it on the blackboard.

"Love." "Sadness." "Anger." These were called out very

slowly, in cramped fashion. I carefully wrote them on the black-board. And I waited for the next one. But, again, nothing came.

Nothing.

"Is that all?" I said. "Is that all the emotional states you can name? I don't believe it."

"Jealousy," said Linda, in the front row.

"Of course," I said, and wrote it on the blackboard.

"Envy," said another woman—"or is that the same thing as jealousy?"

I thought for a moment. What *is* the difference between envy and jealousy—experientially? They are obviously not purely identical, either in usage or experientially. There is a fine shade of difference between them, which I couldn't quite define to myself at the moment. But I did not have time to savor the fact that whatever our emotional life may be, it is capable of some exceedingly subtle gradations. I did not have the time because the whole class suddenly started shouting out the names of emotions—in rapid bursts punctuated by brief silences as though they were reloading, or like flocks of birds that erupt out of a tree and just as suddenly return in one common movement. I frequently had to stop them just in order to write down everything they were saying or in order to make a point.

"Pity."

"Gratitude."

"Foolish."

"Enthralled."

"Disgust."

"Dismayed."

"Suspicious."

"Defiant."

"Misunderstood."

"Proud."

"Depressed."

"Fulfilled."

"Humility."

"Humiliation."

As I was writing these last two words on the blackboard, a bell went off in my mind. Again, I did not have the time to analyze. But I sensed that there was something about the distinction between humility and humiliation that was a key to the whole question of levels of emotion. . . .

"Resentment."

"Enthused."

"Confident."

"Melancholy."

"Depressed."

"Suicidal!"

"Sorrow": this said in a full-bodied, powerfully restrained feminine voice that immediately caught my attention. Here, too, was a key to the question—the difference between sorrow and depression. At that, I myself wrote down the word "grief," as in a flash I remembered what I had immediately felt at the death of each of my parents. And, without turning around, I called out to the class, "Take note of this distinction—between sorrow or grief and what we call 'depression.'"

Like a dam cracking and bursting, the names of emotions spurted out of the class and flooded the room—with much laughter mixed with ever intensifying philosophical interest as the professor, me, often facially and bodily mimicked this or that emotion. As I allowed myself to work with the class in this way, there were moments when I seemed to myself almost to be channeling the human condition itself, the whole life of this poor, amazing puppet called man.

After three-quarters of an hour, the blackboard, stretching across the whole width of the classroom, was entirely filled:

nervous	suspicious	flattered
overwhelmed	defiant	joyous
hungry	misunderstood	irritated
happiness	proud	frustrated
fear	fulfilled	rejected
love	humility	confused
anger	humiliation	cautious
jealousy	resentment	interested
envy	enthused	bored
pity	confident	worthy
gratitude	melancholy	unworthy
foolish	suicidal	grim
enthralled	depressed	horny
disgust	sorrow	reassured
dismayed	grief	scorned

frisky

discouraged

sly

uncertain

sad

bold

awe

sneaky

cheated

self-pity

heartbroken

restive

restless

uninterested

desperate

inauthentic

nauseated

furious

amused

perplexed

alive

heroic

centered

horror

comforted

longing

embarrassed

disheartened

thrilled

defeated

fearful

ashamed

fascinated

agonized

sympathy

great

needy

optimistic

sluggish

empathy

blah

shy

aggressive

mean

forgiving

happy

cowed

numb

brash

compassion

extravagant

disappointed

guilty

tempted

reborn

enthralled

indifferent

youthful

clean

satisfied

enraged

delighted

Jewish

dead

brave

agitated

unfazed

uncomfortable

supported

daunted

troubled

dread

honored

gratified

self-assured

used

cheerful

lost

let down

euphoria

indifferent

determined	rattled	livid
haunted	persecuted	suspicious
sexy	defiled	picked on
scorn	curious	innocent
invincible	burdened	reluctant
tired	envy	exhausted
muddled	resentment	liberated
thrilled	magnanimous	triumphant
intimidated	shocked	dismayed
indecisive	exposed	disgusted
vengeful	infatuated	repelled
greedy	at peace	patient
worried	unappreciated	relieved
surprised	high	Irish
remorse	irate	sadistic
eager	paralyzed	weak
put upon	uncertain	devoted
trapped	called	mad
bested	frenetic	ill at ease
old	timid	shattered
dirty	hostile	bitter
intrigued	murderous	confident
impatient	encouraged	strung out
relaxed	clumsy	ecstatic
unimportant	intoxicated	in love
fulfilled	kind	bliss
strong	wonder	titillated

disrespected	wrath	secure
fed up	indignant	transported
threatened	proud	

It was well past the time to take a ten-minute break, but no one moved. We all stared at the blackboard in absolute silence. We were stunned.

What were we seeing?

Who could have imagined there would be so *many*?

"And that's only the beginning," I said. "We could have named hundreds more!"

I started silently to read each one of them, but slowly, not skipping over any of them.

"Read each of them," I said. "Take your time. Read each one of them and try to catch a glimpse of what each one evokes."

I sat down at an empty chair to the side, in the front row. I wanted to be with the class, looking at the blackboard and the phenomenon in front of us.

Quite a long time passed. Slowly, I began to understand something about emotion that I had never fully realized before. A new question was surfacing in my mind, from what depths I could not then say.

I stood up and went to the blackboard.

"There are many ways that psychologists and philosophers have classified emotions, but I want you to consider one specific aspect, which I believe is of utmost importance in understanding genuine religious emotion." I was reluctant to use the word "religious." That word now seemed too limiting with its conventional associations. I wanted to use instead the word "sacred"—"the sense of the sacred" instead of "religious emotion." But that might have confused things, might have been a distraction. Wasn't what we were dealing with something more *fundamental* than what is conveyed by words like "religious," or even "sacred"? No, not more fundamental, but—I was grasping for a word to explain it to myself before speaking further to the class—more . . . more *intimate*. Yes, more intimate, closer to home, nearer to oneself.

"Look at all these emotions. Don't theorize. Don't force them into categories such as positive and negative, good or bad, pleasant or unpleasant. But just ask yourself—which of these emotions represent something, some impulse or force that brings people or things together—and, on the other hand, which emotions are divisive, which separate people from each other?"

I did not feel that I was saying this well, but I was sure it was leading in the right direction.

I continued: "We'll draw a circle around the emotions that bespeak a movement toward unity, that bring people together with . . . with other people, or that bring people together with . . . something."

The class seemed puzzled . . . understandably.

"Let's just begin," I said. "Let's see. Let's try to find some-thing out about emotions."

I started: " 'Nervous,' " I said, " 'overwhelmed,' 'angry,' 'jeal-ousy'—these emotions are all about *me*, aren't they? All about me in opposition to someone or something other than me, a person or situation. Yes? You agree?" And I went on: " 'Disgust,' 'reassured,' 'confident,'—all about *me*, yes?" I went on: " 'happy,' 'enthralled,' 'thrilled.' "

"But aren't all emotions about me?" said one student, inter-rupting.

I stopped. Instantly, I understood where I was going. "Yes!" I said, surprised by my own vehemence. "But which *me*?"

And there it was—the answer, so quickly, so decisively: "Which *me*?" I continued reading aloud, but now more selec-tively, pausing a little longer after each word.

" 'Embarrassed.' 'Indecisive.' 'Cautious.' " I paused for an extra beat. And then I said:

"Compassion."

It was not my imagination: the posture of nearly everyone in the class changed, became just a little more vertical. Without saying anything, I circled the word "compassion."

I continued: " 'Heartbroken.' 'Self-pity.' 'Defiant.' 'Humili-ated.' " I skipped a beat again, and said:

"Humility."

And again a change in many of the students, something more subtle than before—as though, just a little, people moved . . .

back into themselves. This time I did say something as I circled the word:

"These two words, 'humiliation' and 'humility,' so alike in appearance—are worlds apart in what they mean, in the experience they refer to."

At that, the Irish brogue of Brennan O'Brien rose in the air like the song of a bird:

"And I know very well what it is that you mean, Professor Needleman!"

"Can you say?"

"I most certainly can, Professor. When I am humiliated," he began, "it is my ego that suffers. But when I am humbled, it is . . . it is . . ."

Mr. O'Brien was suddenly in difficulty. He seemed suddenly to have lost his voice.

Everyone was waiting for him to finish his thought.

Mr. O'Brien cannot find the words to say. He is struggling. His craggy face has become as red as his hair. I make a move to suggest a word . . . he sharply waves me off. His eyes meet mine. His eyes are moist. Never have I seen him like that. He is struggling with something more than words. And he is not embarrassed at all—that much is clear. He doesn't care at all that the class is anxiously waiting for him. Again I am moved to help him and again he waves me off.

I realize that he is struggling to be true to something he loves—or . . . *and* . . . something that loves *him*. And in that moment, sensing his unique inner struggle, I think to myself: "I love this man." It is impossible not to love a man or woman in the moment they are struggling for truth.

Finally, his state changes enough to allow him, with difficulty, to find words.

"When I am humbled," he says, "my heart . . . relaxes. I feel . . . a . . . solemn freedom."

Once again, we are all silenced.

After a few minutes, I announce the break. The students file out of the room.

After ten minutes or so, most of the students were back in their chairs and I went to the blackboard, knowing very clearly what I now wished to say about the emotions. Because there was less than a half-hour left until the end of the class I started by simply circling the following words without comment:

compassion
humility
wonder
sorrow
grief
empathy
remorse
shattered

"I believe," I said, "that these emotions and those like them bring us an entirely different sense of self, a different feeling of 'I.' Look and see if this is so: a different 'I am.' In almost all the other emotions on the blackboard, almost all the other emotions in our everyday life, it is the ego that is involved, not the 'I am.' Let me say this using more traditional language. You all know by now that many of the spiritual traditions of the world speak of the Self—with a capital *S*, and differentiate it from the self with a small *s*. The Self and the self. Or, we could say, *I* and *me*. Behind the me, behind the self, myself, there exists, unseen, unknown, the Self. We live our lives almost entirely from the self, the me. But occasionally in our lives the Self—or a fleeting glimpse in the direction of the Self—is given to us to experience.

"These are the non-egoistic emotions. I will say this quickly now because we don't have much more time today. The non-egoistic emotions bring with them a completely different sense of I. Deeply quiet. Strong, very, but with none of the violence that passes for strength in our usual lives. We speak of strong emotions, such as anger or rage or avidity or fear. But what kind of strength is it?

"In any case, these non-egoistic emotions have been called the 'impersonal emotions.' This is a very helpful phrase, as we shall see. But it can also be a bit misleading. They are impersonal only in the sense that they are not in the service of strengthening the grip of egoism, the conditioned psychological me. On the contrary, these 'impersonal emotions' bring with them a movement toward the real I, the Self, the profoundly intimate and powerful *I am*. When they are active in us, we sense that this is our real identity, our genuine I.

"We do not have much time left today, so I will only say one thing more—and it is very important for understanding the meaning of God in the Eastern religions. It used to be that many academicians and theologians differentiated Eastern religion from Western by referring to the Hindu notion of the absolute God as an 'impersonal' force, whereas our Western religions tend to speak of God as a person, a personal God.

"But this is a false distinction. The point is that, as with the impersonal emotions, which are impersonal only in that they are not egoistic but in reality are deeply personal in that they carry the deeper intrinsic reality of I am, the Self—just so the fundamental cosmic reality of the Eastern traditions carries with it the deeper sense of I, of Self-ness, which, to the untutored mind seems to be 'cold.' It is not cold."

I glanced up at the clock. The class was running way over. I had to hurry. I had to make the main point of everything that had been tried.

"Please listen to this," I said to the class, "and we'll discuss it next time. The main point I wish to make is that at its higher levels, consciousness is intrinsically personal. Conscious energy is intrinsically what we might call *I-ness*. You could say, reality has the ultimate property of *I-am-ness*. I-am-ness without form, without incarnation, emptiness in the most fertile sense of the word; silence in its most fertile sense—reality anterior to manifestation, to form. What the Kabbalah calls the hidden God beyond God; Brahman anterior to the creation of the universe, Meister Eckhart's pure Godness . . . Plato's . . ."

But I was going too fast, I was racing, jamming ideas together, bewildering everyone. I stopped cold, and smiled. And laughed. The whole class seemed to exhale in relief. And everyone gathered their books and papers together.

"See you Thursday," I said.

The classroom emptied out. Everyone left except for one person. I went over to her.

Part Four

CHAPTER SEVENTEEN

"God Sends the Wind, but Man Must Raise the Sail"

In order to think about God in your presence, my reader, under your eyes, I have so far written about a childhood encounter with great nature and the infinite universe; I have written about my encounter with the incomprehensible fact of death; with my father's God; and, as I grew older, about my encounter with the call to an independent mind—that is, the call of self-sufficient philosophical reasoning and its sincere worship, not of God but of logic and experience.

I have written of my discovery of the esoteric roots of Judaism, the religion of my childhood, from which I fled, but which sought me out and wrestled me to the ground and about which I could now say, like my namebearer, the Biblical Jacob: God was in that place and I knew it not.

I have written of my discovery of Christianity, as one wave after another of the meaning of Jesus Christ washed over me from many directions—from the impassioned theologians of antiquity and the twentieth century; from the tear-stained ecstasies of the early Fathers of the desert; from the divine words of Meister Eckhart and the unknown author of *The Cloud of Unknowing*,[56] and, yes, even from my old "enemy," Saint Augustine, the pages of whose *Confessions* I once spitefully set on fire one by one.

I have written about my encounter with Zen Buddhism and its masterful interpreter D. T. Suzuki. Or should I speak of my experience with Dr. Suzuki by calling to mind what a Zen monk once said about his teacher: "I owe everything to my teacher—because he taught me nothing"?

And I have written of my encounter with Tibetan Buddhism in the person of my beloved friend Lobsang Lhalungpa, who, so far as I am able to understand such things, seemed to incarnate the compassionate being of Tibet's great saint, Milarepa, whose autobiography a group of us were translating with him over a period of several years.

I have written about my work with students, trying to speak about the question of God to and from the "I am" in each of us, rather than to and from the protected, artificial "self."

And, finally, I have written about my discovery and rediscovery of the Gurdjieff teaching, which has been the sustaining inner companion of my adult life up to the present moment. I wish and feel morally obliged to speak here about how it has helped me to begin to understand, not just mentally or emotionally but through undeniable experience, what God is.

Through the help of that teaching, I have understood that God cannot be known or approached beyond a certain point by the ordinary self. The awakening of the true "I am" is necessary; and it is this that has been forgotten. It is this "metaphysical amnesia" that explains why throughout history there is endless conflict and horror, not only with respect to religion but in all aspects of human life. It is this awakening to the "I am," toward which the spiritual teachings of the world have tried to lead man, sometimes from very, very far and through labyrinthine paths of ideas, art, symbolism, manners and customs, and precise ritual forms—and, above all, through the example of the lives and being of men and women who have greatly discovered what and who they are.

I began this book by claiming that to think about God is to the human soul what breathing is to the human body. I am saying that genuine thought about God both demands and supports a definite change of consciousness within oneself. A definite glimpse of the experience of "I am." I am saying that almost all of the contradictions, conflicts, arguments, complaints about what God is, or to whom He belongs, or why His messengers act in the sometimes incomprehensible way they act—I am saying that such thought about God can lead nowhere when it is conducted without the accompanying inner search for one's Self, one's own unique soul, one's own "I am."

One cannot think about God in the same way that one thinks about scientific problems, psychological theories, or logical proofs. There are no ultimate logical proofs for the existence of God—it is just as Kant and others, such as Kierkegaard, have said. And that is because reason cannot go toward God without at the same time seeking the presence in oneself of the real I. Likewise, one cannot have genuine faith in God without the experience, if only for a moment, of one's real I. Everything else that passes for faith—when it is not simply fantasy or self-deception—is a preparation for faith, often a necessary preparation as becomes evident when, for example, the bottom falls out in our life, or everything is lost, and then an individual experiences the faith that until then, unknown to him or her, had been no more or less than a preparatory, guiding hypothesis. In all such cases of the experience of real faith a man or woman is also experiencing the real I, even if he or she does not give it that name.

B ut now, concerning Gurdjieff.
     It was after glimpsing the unique goodness of the man Gurdjieff in Thomas de Hartmann's book *Our Life with Mr. Gurdjieff,* and after rediscovering the force of his ideas in Ouspensky's book *In Search of the Miraculous,* that I found my way back to the Gurdjieff teaching as it applied to my own life. I was at that time still a young assistant professor of philosophy.

I was deeply struck by the fact that the word or even the general idea of God did not seem to have a place in Gurdjieff's teaching. It never entered the books I was reading, except for its relatively rare usage—in ways that for many years I could neither digest nor even perceive—in Gurdjieff's own writings. Nor did it enter at all into the conversations I began having with the group of men and women who were studying his teaching and trying to put it into practice. Nor did it enter into the remarkable explanations of the man, John Pentland, who had been one of the direct pupils of Gurdjieff and who from time to time came to support the inner work of these men and women. I will speak about him in a moment. My debt to him is incalculable.

The absence of the idea of God, and the absence of the word itself, hovered like an unknown presence throughout the initial years of my engagement with this teaching.

Like a strength without a name.

Like a secret mountain.

At the same time, my awakening interest in religion developed as I have earlier described it—fueling my work of teaching about Judaism and Christianity and, soon after, about the religions of Asia, Buddhism, Hinduism, and also Islam, which had always felt alien, but which was now revealing itself to me through its mystics and Sufis. But although my appreciation of religious ideas grew and deepened, there remained a wall of separation between my work as a professor of philosophy and what I was now personally discovering about human life, my *own* human life, including its unimagined cosmic, meta-physical dimensions. On one side of the wall, the philosopher thought and spoke with an ever increasing sense of discovery and conviction about great philosophical questions and about the many spiritual and mystical traditions of mankind. Yet on the other side of the wall, totally separated from the life of the philosopher, the student of the Gurdjieff teaching was having vividly penetrating impressions of a struggle that was illuminating my life like an entirely new sun rising in an entirely new sky.

Let me be clear. At the level of philosophical ideas, almost from the beginning, the Gurdjieff ideas soon began to help me to expand my understanding and appreciation of the spiritual teachings of the world. The wall, the separation I am speaking of, was much subtler, much deeper down.

And I now have the language to be clear about this. *In my depths I remained an atheist.* Touched as I was by the great truths about the human condition that the Gurdjieff teaching had articulated, I could not say, nor even want to say, that I knew what God was or that He, She, or It existed. Deep in my depths there still existed, seemingly undiscovered and untouched, the cave of absence where, as I have said, Kant slept and where, in a far-off corner, that child of eight years also slept, along with his vision of a million stars in the dark sky. And I am now convinced that, in my case at least, the Gurdjieff teaching could never have flowed down into my life without its initial near silence about "God." The fact is that even all my deepening appreciation of the world's religious teachings never touched or even came near to that cave of absence, that metaphysical subconsciousness where the atheist lived.

Was *that* what Gurdjieff meant when he said his teachings were directed to the subconscious? Is it because down in the subconscious depths, the crisis of our civilization is the absence of the divine, uncorrupted impulses of hope, love, and faith?

I think the soul of our whole civilization is asleep in that same cave.

To continue: For years, much as I appreciated the idea of self-remembering as an idea, I was never sure that I actually experienced it—experienced it, that is, as the result of an effort of inner struggle. But what I did experience more and more—and this alone lit up my world—was the value of the struggle itself, the struggle to see oneself as one is, stripping away more and more of the illusions of the socially conditioned self-identity, experiencing the bittersweet taste of simultaneous freedom (of awareness) and the inner slavery which was the object of awareness; the bittersweet taste of the freedom of seeing and, simultaneously, the helplessness of what is seen. The simultaneous hope of consciousness and the hopelessness of self-delusion.

I had never heard or ever imagined that such an inner struggle existed as possibility, *my* possibility. The Gurdjieff teaching includes this struggle within the word *work*, work on oneself. Nothing in all the books I had read about the disciplines and inner experiences of the Christian mystics, or the Zen Buddhist monks, or the followers of the Indian gurus, or the Hasidic teachers and their pupils—nothing in all that material prepared me for the actual experience of this specific quality of inner self-effort. Nor had I been prepared by many years of closely reading the master of inwardness, Kierkegaard; or the prophet of self-overcoming, Nietzsche; or even by Plato's Socrates, our common god of self-examination. Later, I was able to see these heroes of my younger mind very differently and more accurately. But that was only after years of exposure to that unknown capacity in myself, in man, that can try to do what Gurdjieff so often and in so many words speaks of as man's being-obligation—namely, the metaphysical duty to awaken *I am* from the sleep that blankets human life.

I soon realized one very important aspect of these personal impressions of that capacity in myself to undertake these efforts. I realized that they were made possible for me by many external factors. One of these factors was, of course, the ideas in the books I was reading. As I have already recounted, it was while reading Ouspensky's book that I was *given* a glimpse of Selfhood. But from the ideas alone I did not receive and could not have received the experience of my human capacity to struggle—that is, the hidden human capacity intentionally to cultivate the twofold receptivity to the experience of the Self and the impressions of that in us which obstructs or counterfeits this experience. And I soon saw the reasons why it was impossible for me—and perhaps for anyone—to discover this capacity in oneself from books alone or by oneself alone without direct help and guidance.

This point bears emphasizing. Most people during their lives are *given* experiences of what can be called self-remembering, or the experience of *I am* at one or another level. Such experiences are common in childhood, but they can also occur at any time, sometimes simply out of nowhere, and more often during special extreme moments of danger; or joy; or grief; or wonder; or remorse; or deep and sudden loss or disappointment. In such moments a man or woman may come closer to becoming the human being he or she wishes to be— capable of love, compassion, inner peace, intelligence, resourceful action and often uncommon strength. That is, such experiences are like messages from our own real Self. Messages that say: "I am you. Let me enter your life."

But rare are the moments when one is given to understand *how* to struggle or how to live in a way that makes us, body and soul, available to such experiences. For such experiences, were we to become more available to them, would eventually transform us.

In the words, or so I have heard, of Saint Augustine, "God sends the wind, but man must raise the sail."[57]

The ideas, then, were one, but only one, of the factors that made it possible for me to discover the experience of my capacity for this precise inner work. But—mercifully, as it now is clear to me—nothing about "God" was as yet experienced or contemplated.

The second essential factor was the conditions under which the men and women studying this teaching came together in order to work together. Like many sensible people, I was always allergic to "groups" and always ran toward the exit when invited or, even worse, when "required" to join anything. However, I now found that there was something about the atmosphere of the Gurdjieff community that touched me in the way one can be touched, for example, by certain traditional music, which on the surface may seem uninteresting when compared to much of the music that excites or inspires people, but which, when one brings to it a certain inner need, both quietens the mind and pierces the heart.

But it is impossible for me to try honorably to speak further about this second essential factor without first speaking about the third of the essential factors that made it possible for me to experience the capacity for inner work, and which eventually led me to the taste of certainty about God.

This third factor is the presence of people or an individual who can serve as a guide along the way to Self-knowledge. And here I am obliged and wholeheartedly wish to say something about John Pentland.

Lord Pentland—a title he had inherited from his father—was of Scottish ancestry and for many years had been a pupil of P. D. Ouspensky. Not long after Ouspensky's death in 1947, he became a pupil of Gurdjieff and worked closely under his guidance until Gurdjieff's death in 1949. Thereafter, he emerged as a leading figure in the transmission of the Gurdjieff teaching in the United States.

Lord Pentland was a man of striking appearance—lean and vibrant, with commanding eyes and voice and Lincolnesque physical presence.

The most essential thing I wish to say about this remarkable man concerns a certain effect he had, not only on me, but on very many others. While I believe it is the most essential thing about his work as a guide, it is also the most difficult to convey. And the reason it is so difficult is not only because it involves intimate psychological aspects of an individual's inner world, aspects that simply evaporate or set themselves on fire on the printed page. What I am speaking of goes far beyond that. What I am speaking of is the evocation of a certain emotion that is, I would say, all but unknown to humanity in the ordinary, everyday conduct of our lives. And, I would say further, it is the awakening of this feeling that lies at the heart of Gurdjieff's work as a teacher and guide.

That emotion is what Gurdjieff called "remorse of conscience." When that feeling breaks through the surface of one's awareness, the experience is enormous and unbearable. For an ordinary man or woman, it is the deepest possible experience of the truth about oneself. Nothing else in oneself can withstand it. All pretense, all "self-esteem," all sense of achievement, all egoism, all "plans for the future," all emotional reckoning and accounting about oneself and one's relations, all anxious guilt trips—all, everything, melts before genuine remorse of conscience, if one allows the experience in. One's head bows in acceptance, solemn sorrow, before the truth of what one is. If it is possible to speak of degrees of this experience, then at the far end of the scale would be what Christianity offers an individual in front of the crucifixion of God—not by the Romans or the Jews, and not just by man in general (though that is an essential aspect), but by oneself, by me. But the "me" here is a cosmic fact as well as a personal individual entity, myself.

Gurdjieff's remorse of conscience has nothing in common, except in words, with what ordinary usage calls by that name. In fact, what we usually call conscience is, so Gurdjieff taught, a form of escape from the truth of our being, escape into the illusion that one is able to be otherwise. No power of the ordinary psyche can conquer what genuine remorse of conscience reveals. But, he tells us, only in the fire of this remorse can the new man be awakened and take his place in human life. Mercifully—for me, at least—in Ouspensky's account Gurdjieff never uses religious language to refer to the force that can enter man through the acceptance of the experience of genuine remorse. However, in his own writings, and in other accounts of his teaching, he speaks of it as the voice of God.

CHAPTER EIGHTEEN

Attention

I wish now to speak about the community which made it possible for me to verify, through experience, things that I had never in my life believed could be capable of verification. This will perhaps enable me finally to say the unsayable about the experience of God. I wish with all my heart to succeed in this.

It so happens that this was the Gurdjieff community—as it existed in San Francisco, New York and Paris.

Before going further, however, some background about Gurdjieff and his teaching is needed.

Of Gurdjieff's early life we know only what he has revealed in the autobiographical portions of his own writings, notably *Meetings with Remarkable Men*.[58] He was born, probably in 1866, to a Greek father and an Armenian mother in Alexandropol (now Gumri), Armenia, a region where Eastern and Western cultures mixed and often clashed. He relates how, as a boy, listening to his father recite myths and stories that were part of an age-old oral tradition, he had felt there was a profound wisdom embodied in them, the keys to which had been lost.

His wish to understand life soon led him to investigate

everything he came across that might help him: orthodox religion, fortune-tellers, hypnotism, the teachings of modern science. But since everything he studied was full of contradictions, he determined to rediscover the lost wisdom himself. Bringing others together with him in a loosely organized group and overcoming countless hardships and dangers, he pursued his quest for some twenty years (1894–1912), seeking out holy men and inaccessible monasteries, mainly in Central Asia and the Middle East.

What was the result? Certainly, far more than a mere accumulation of texts, rituals and spiritual practices. His own subsequent life is strong evidence that he had found what he was searching for—a complete reintegration of the lost and forgotten wisdom within his own experience and understanding, which he then labored to express in language understandable to modern man. And which he devoted his life to transmitting to others, creating for future generations psychological and communal conditions for inner work unique in the modern world. It is those conditions, altogether constituting what has since ancient times been called an "oral tradition," that have to some extent survived him, and upon which, in large measure, depends the future influence of his teaching in the life of our era.

Thus it was that Gurdjieff appeared in Moscow in 1912, bringing with him a teaching unlike anything known or heard of in the modern world. Both the man himself and his ideas about "all and everything" continue to astonish the mind and mysteriously touch the heart, or else remain invisible behind the curtain of assumptions about reality and human nature that govern the thought of almost all men and women in the modern world.

In nearly every aspect of thought, Gurdjieff's ideas bring an unimaginably new perspective, which on closer examination at the same time echoes something enormously living and ancient.

His vision of the universe is of an all-embracing organic, purposeful reality both "horizontally" and "vertically" vast—vast, that is, both quantitatively in space and form and qualitatively in levels and degrees of conscious energy.

His vision of man on earth is of a being created to fulfill a great universal purpose of conscious love and intelligence who instead lives and dies mortally asleep to what he is meant to be.

Within this twofold vision, Gurdjieff's thought encompasses in startling and often verifiable detail the history and fate of our planet Earth; the origins of life and of man; the rise and fall of civilizations; the purpose of art and its widespread degeneration; the tragedy of education; the structure and function of the human organism—and much else: the causes of war, the accelerating violation of the natural world, the illusions of technology, and—ultimately—the outline of the single thread of possibility that remains for us.

The shock of his ideas consists not only in the newness of their form, but also in their explanatory power. Many of his ideas both contradict certain fundamental assumptions of modern science and at the same time foreshadow many of its empirical discoveries about man, nature and the universe. But the deeper shock is what his teaching indicates to each individual about his or her own personal life. No doubt in some measure like the man himself, his writings and the accounts by his pupils shake our entire sense of ourselves while at the same time touching the last remaining nerve of hope within us.

But his essential legacy will surely be judged principally by the quality of the men and women who worked most closely with him and, further, by the inner quality of those who have come after them. It is necessary now to look more closely at what kind of human development we are speaking of when we say that the aim of his teaching is *the creation of people*.

What does that mean—the creation of people? For myself at least, it is here that the whole question of the existence and nature of God is hidden. The accumulated experiences and reasoning of my own life had shown me, semiconsciously, that in order to know Truth, or God, it cannot help past a certain point to look in philosophical proofs or sacred books or at art or even at nature and the sky in all their grandeur. It was only when I was systematically and repeatedly touched by a specific influence that could at one and the same moment be physically sensed, emotionally perceived, and mentally acknowledged that, after some years, something or someone stirred in that cave of absence—in that metaphysical subconsciousness which since childhood had remained walled off from my everyday existence and understanding. I have come to the conclusion that this quality of influence can exist, and in our modern culture perhaps can only exist, through the intentions and actions of inwardly developed people.

Let me put it bluntly, leaving aside some important qualifications and exceptions: It is only in and through people, inwardly developed men and women, that God can exist and act in the world of man on earth. Bluntly speaking, the proof for the existence of God is the existence of people who are inhabited by and who manifest God.

Furthermore, this proof, this evidence, is strictly speaking not perceived simply by means of reasoning or emotionally reacting to such people. This evidence is perceived by means of what their presence evokes in oneself. Our society is not like certain cultures that may possibly have existed in other lands or eras in which the presence or even the idea of a higher purpose or consciousness (call it God or Truth or Nirvana, etc.) inhabits the very air one breathes—that is to say, where language, social customs, ritual forms, scientific discovery, music, art, contain influences that have originated through inwardly developed people. Gurdjieff obviously understood this very well and therefore sought to create a kind of subculture in which more-conscious influences could support the exercise of a man or woman's inherent, but undeveloped, capacity to work on him- or herself. Modern culture by itself could never offer that overall support.

Many such communities—schools, "brotherhoods"—have no doubt emerged at critical points and places throughout history, although it is difficult from the outside to know which have been authentic and which imitative. Here and now, such a community may be thought of as a subculture in that almost all the personal relationships within the community are meant to exist solely for the sake of supporting the impulse of remembering and returning to the "I am," the Self. Such a culture or communal organization is based on values unlike the values underpinning the modern world as a whole, which despite surface claims to the contrary are rooted in egoism, greed, fear and the pleasure principle.

One essential aspect of this subculture must be emphasized. It does not and was apparently never meant to exist apart from our modern world, such as it is. Examples of this kind of community can be found throughout history. I have heard such a community spoken of as "a monastery in the midst of life." That is to say, the aim of the inner work involved the capacity for a full-hearted engagement in the everyday life of the world, culminating in the capacity to love and serve the genuine needs of man and the earth.

These special conditions comprising a metaphysical subculture, taken together, constitute what I have called the second essential factor that enabled me to discover my own capacity for inner work.

But here is an essential point. These special conditions in my case were in their all-important specific details created and maintained by Lord Pentland, whose own mission was, along with the nucleus of other pupils who had worked directly with

Gurdjieff, to transmit the teaching to others. It was his direct influence that gave these "special conditions" their force and effectiveness. From the very beginning of my contact with this group of men and women, I recognized as coming from Lord Pentland something I had never seen or felt in any human being.

I wish to be quite clear here because upon this quality that I sensed in him lies the basis in my own life for the conviction I have formed about the question "What is God?"

What was it about him? As the years passed, I had more and more contact with him. And more and more I felt and sensed his uniqueness—not only in him, but in myself as a result of contact with him. From the very beginning I knew that he cared most of all for the inner development of all the men and women who worked with him. But I couldn't at first find the word or fact that would designate this ability or personal care he had for others. There was something paradoxically impersonal and mysteriously warm at the same time; something both rigorous and unpredictable.

And also something extraordinarily intelligent. As an academician and professor, I felt secure (perhaps foolishly) in my ability to judge another person's mind. Perhaps in my better moments I would never pretend to judge another person's spiritual development or sincerity of intention, but I knew a good mind when I saw it. His was by far the best I had ever encountered.

But that was not yet the most essential thing about him. It was something emanating from him. In order to communicate the nature of that something essential in him, I am obliged again to be quite personal. Some of the details of what I am about to say may apply only to myself and my particular subjectivity. At the same time, I am certain, quite certain, that in its essence it applies to every man and woman in the modern world. Only in this way will I be able truly to offer my present understanding of what it was about him that was so remarkable and to offer a precise name for it.

I will begin by saying that what I experienced from Lord Pentland was an attitude toward me that I had never encountered from anyone or even imagined. He seemed bewilderingly unimpressed by almost everything I said or did, and yet at the same time he seemed greatly interested in me. He responded to my questions often by showering down insights based on the Gurdjieff ideas that were clairvoyantly relevant to my personal life and which one after another erased or eclipsed everything I thought I had understood. I—Professor Jacob Needleman, who could, so to say, hold my own more or less with Plato, Hume, Kant and even the God of the Bible—I could not hold my own with the mind of this strangely intelligent man. Almost every time I spoke with him I experienced—on my very own turf of the intellect—the simultaneous deflation of my mind and exhilaration of the taste of Truth, the glimpse of a higher understanding. That was one aspect of my repeated encounters with Lord Pentland.

But it was only one aspect and by no means the most important one. Even more important was the emotional atmosphere that he created in the community of people who came together to put the teaching into practice. I have already mentioned the awakening of conscience that is one of the far and fundamental aims of work, an experience which Lord Pentland, with no mean hand, projected into the life of the whole community. I am speaking here about an atmosphere of suffering that, overall, had no basic negativity about it. On the contrary. A suffering in front of the awareness of one's own illusions about oneself and in front of one's own egoism, awkwardness, fear, sentimentality—a suffering about one's own essential failure to be—to be . . . to be what? To fail . . . how? By what . . . measure? What standard? And the sharing, the communality of this suffering of seeing oneself and, at the same time, detecting the subtle background sense of liberation, impersonal liberation, a shared community of faintly liberated men and women, always falling away into the sleep of humanity, and at the same time, struggling to embrace the utter truth about oneself, the truth that included the light of possible liberation always waiting in the back of one's being, so to speak. Almost one hundred percent of the men and women there, myself included, experienced this atmosphere in and around Lord Pentland as a quality of—I have no choice but to use this word now—a quality of love.

With surgical precision the conditions he created, and the personal "something" that he emanated, put one just an inch or so in front of the fundamental illusions about oneself within which one conducted one's ordinary life and which together formed one's sense of everyday identity. Within an inch of the final acknowledgment of what was right before one's eyes, the final receiving of the impressions being offered as a special kind of unknown food uniquely for human beings, impressions of the truth about oneself which, as we later understood, were precisely what was needed for the growth of one's being. But that final inch always had to be taken by oneself, by an act of one's will and intention. Nothing in this sphere could ever be forced. This is what I have been speaking of as the capacity to struggle, to work. The struggle was not against anything but one's unwillingness to see the truth, a struggle supported eventually by the knowledge that this seeing was the first step toward the liberation one dreamt of, the first step in the movement toward becoming a real human being.

All this was suffering that radiated joy: the joy of voluntary suffering in front of truth. Not the suffering of the egoism, but closer to the honorable suffering of the human condition—not neurotic suffering, but on the way to essence-sorrow; a unique suffering and struggle to see and accept one's distance from what one was meant to be and from what one imagined oneself to be. Again and again, on the individual and communal level, Lord Pentland brought his pupils into the honorableness of the struggle to pass from nonexistence, humanly speaking, to being. And each individual man and woman, in his or her own way, loved this man and trusted his guidance.

One had read such things about how the pupils of Gurdjieff deeply loved and trusted him, even though many outside observers saw nothing they could value and created many fantastic rumors.

Now I can use the word that, I believe, accurately—at least in part—names what it was that Lord Pentland emanated. And it is this "something" that will lead us in thought, as it led me in experience, to the idea and the experience of God.

That "something" is *attention*.

How to understand this mystery? For this it is necessary to speak about the person to whom Lord Pentland himself turned for guidance—Jeanne de Salzmann.

CHAPTER NINETEEN

What Is God?

It was from Jeanne de Salzmann that I first heard the word "God" used alongside comments about the fundamental aims of the inner work. And when I first heard that word, in the intense conditions under which I heard it, it was as though for one second the wall between my two worlds was penetrated. It was as though something electric passed between those worlds, those two halves of myself: the teacher, writer, man-in-the-world, and the inner seeker intimately and protectively moving toward self-remembering independently of any religious language or beliefs. Suddenly, for one second and no more, the person, the *I*, that had studied and taught about religion and philosophy, the I with so many memories associated with the idea and the word "God"—including memories half-buried and memories still influencing my everyday sense of identity—suddenly, in a flash, that person, that *I* sensed somewhere in my body the thrill of a possible unity I could never have expected or known about. A glimpse, a lightning-flash, an unknown physical vibration of *thought*.

And then it was gone. But from that moment, the wall between my two lives began little by little to take on a completely different quality. The wall remained, but I now began to feel it as necessary, more like a membrane in a living being separating two systems of functioning, both of which were necessary to life.

Was it really true? Was this teaching really about God after all? The very thought drifted down into me like soft rain in a parched land.

Before his death in 1949, Gurdjieff entrusted the task of transmitting the teaching to his chief pupil, Jeanne de Salzmann, who had originally come to Gurdjieff with her husband in Tbilisi, Georgia, in 1919, in the midst of Gurdjieff's long exodus with his small band of pupils from the violence and chaos of the Russian Revolution. This exodus, so poignantly described in the book of Thomas de Hartmann, ended in France in 1922, where Gurdjieff took up permanent residence.

A gifted student of dance and movement, Jeanne de Salzmann continuously worked closely with Gurdjieff during the rest of his life and was responsible for helping him develop what has come to be known as the Movements, spiritually remarkable dances and bodily exercises unique in the modern world. But of even more importance, she was able to carry forward the force of his teaching to the circle of pupils who survived him, and who themselves would soon be traveling the world to help guide the slowly increasing numbers of men and women who felt drawn to the Gurdjieff teaching. Lord Pentland had been one of that circle.

I first came into contact with Madame de Salzmann, as she was called, in New York sometime in November or December 1967. I was on academic leave that year, working at Union Theological Seminary under a grant from the Society for Religion in Higher Education. My research project involved a study of the concept of the authentic self in early Christian thought as set against its Judaic background. I was also a guest lecturer in the Philosophy Department of Columbia University.

I had chosen to spend the year in New York not only for academic reasons, but also in order to attend meetings at the Gurdjieff Foundation in New York. The New York Foundation was Lord Pentland's base and I eagerly looked forward to a year of attending meetings led by him. I had heard that Madame de Salzmann came from Paris to visit the New York house every year, but to me she was still only a rarely spoken name.

That was in 1967, and over the years I met with her many times.

Her presence was truly remarkable. And what she evoked in me even while she spoke was also remarkable: A sensation of silence as a sacred energy.

Her words were simple and direct and carried immense authority.

Again and again she used the word "attention" in a way that I had never heard it used before. I had already come to realize that in this teaching the word meant far more than what it means in ordinary usage, referring to far more than a simple mental or cerebral mechanism. So much so that it sometimes seemed to be the linchpin of the whole teaching about man in the universal world.

But I really did not know where to go with this, what to make of this fascinating idea that the quality of man's attention is the key to the meaning of our lives and the possible growth of our being. How was one to understand the colossal weight and importance carried by this seemingly cool, thin word?

What is man? What is the sense and meaning of our existence on earth? Why do we live? And die? How was one to understand that the answer to such questions was somehow embedded in the hidden depths of "attention"?

It is true that I had already seen *something* of the importance of attention during my attempts at the practice of self-observation. I could understand through experience that our lives are what they are in large part because of the weakness and passivity of our attention. We are *taken*, our attention is taken, swallowed, by our streams of automatic thought; we constantly disappear into our emotional reactions; we are taken by our fears and desires, our pleasures and pains, by our daydreams and imaginary worries. And, being *taken*, we no longer exist as I, myself, here. We do not live our lives; we *are lived* and we may eventually die without ever having awakened to what we really are—without having lived.

Once this was pointed out and brought home through

experience, it was not difficult to see the importance of attention in this context. This and more: Within this process of self-observation there were certain brief flashes of another kind or level of attention accompanied by a new sensation of existence, as when a two-dimensional figure suddenly becomes three-dimensional, that is to say, really existing. But I didn't exactly think of it as a new attention . . . I thought of it, loosely, as "consciousness" or "self-remembering." The word "attention" would have seemed too small. And yet, the word carried something uniquely intimate, that is to say, uniquely in my power. Consciousness was a state of being—something perhaps that a man could aspire to, but without any clear sense of what means one could employ. Attention pointed to something much closer to hand. It was there; I had it—to whatever small degree. It was in me, in my mind, in my selfness. I could put it on this or that, or I could let it go. But it was mine, it was mine. This small, thin capacity, this tiny spark of uniquely human freedom.

It was there, it was me, it was Jerry. Jerry had thoughts, ideas, he had feelings, he had memories, he had a body. But was any of that *me, I*?

I am my attention. Everything else is given, is not *mine*. But what, exactly, is this uniquely human capacity which I do not understand or really value? I value something I call my knowledge, my skills, my actions; I feel remorse also for my actions, or feel pleased by them; I admire or dislike my body, my strength or weakness. But my attention? It *is* I! How could I fail to value it? How could I have lived without consciously recognizing it as the heart of what I am, the mind of what I am? But where does it come from? Is it biological? Does it form in the womb? Is it governed by the laws of heredity? Like a tissue, an instinct, a neural pattern?

Or does it enter our being from quite another source?

Merely seeing myself as I was, as my experience in the practice of self-observation showed me, was surprisingly difficult but also, paradoxically, surprisingly simple. My efforts at this practice presented me with a seemingly illogical fact. Looking at something in myself without trying to change it or judge it was itself a force, an energy that had an action upon what was seen. And indeed sometimes it had a transforming action upon my entire state of being. Such was the power of pure attention.

Self-observation was not simply an instrument for acquiring information about myself that I could later use to change something. Self-observation was not like scientific observation of nature, in which one tries not to disturb the object observed. No, I began to understand that self-observation was itself an instrument of change, but change of a kind one could never have imagined or expected. Change in the direction of human sensitivity, presence, being. For a moment only, and then gone. But what a precious moment! What a precious indication that it was indeed possible to cultivate another, more humanly meaningful state of being! At the same time, such self-observation had the frequent result of bringing one face-to-face with the inner helplessness which permeated one's life. And seeing that helplessness brought the deeper wish to work, to try, to understand this poor puppet who called itself by my name.

So, yes, I did understand something of the power of attention, but I hadn't yet really understood its huge significance in all of human life, my own and the life of mankind. And I certainly had no idea that it could open the door to the experience of God. The philosophers had never spoken of this—or if some did, they never called it by that name. Their concepts may have been powerful, and I could recognize their great insights about ideas, ethics, and the human mind. But nothing of what they said, even at their greatest, even my dearly loved Plato and Kant and Kierkegaard and Nietzsche—none of them pointed me toward that intimate I-ness, that intimate *myself* which I had begun to recognize under the word attention. Attention was the mystery in broad daylight! It was there and it was hidden, it was I, and it had the power to feed me, to grow me in a way that all the great ideas of the past and present never had. Later, certainly, I saw things a little differently; I saw in the shadows of Plato's words, in the fleeting shadow of Socrates' influence, in the corners of Kant's great mind, hidden perhaps even from himself, I saw the meaning of attention. And in the writings of the religious masters of Christianity and Judaism, at first I could see nothing of what this word meant, until . . . And then: what a fool I had been! It was there all along! Or was it? Did they know it? Did they know that fleeting something, that ultimately intimate force within the mind that is the key to seeing oneself for what one is and perhaps the key to becoming what one is meant to be?

Yes, attention was the elusive obvious, the invisible mountain around which light curves so that the mountain is invisible and untouchable—until, as René Daumal wrote, the mountain chooses to touch us, to draw us toward itself only because we wish to find it, to *be*.[59]

Yes, I had big, broad hints about the importance of attention. But nothing of all that had prepared me for what Madame de Salzmann was trying to show us.

Or, rather, yes—it had prepared me very well for the shock of recognition. What I had already learned about attention was something I really had learned from myself, from my own being—not something I had simply heard about or read about.

Therefore I can say that my experience showed me something critical about attention and at the same time showed me how little I understood about it. But all this was my own knowing. The conditions I had been given allowed me to learn this for myself, in my mind, in my body, in my heart. It was as Gurdjieff had said: there is such a thing as essence-knowing. Knowing from one's own being. All the rest was secondhand furniture in the acquired personality that could be changed in half an hour. How could all our philosophy and religion and psychology have missed the centrality of this capacity called attention, even undeveloped as it was in us?

So, when I say that nothing had prepared me for what

Madame de Salzmann was trying to bring, it is both true and untrue at the same time. I was prepared, yet not prepared, for the immensity of what she was trying to bring, not as an idea, however great and however revolutionary beyond all anticipation in our modern world. She was in fact working to bring it into the flesh-and-blood lives of the men and women who wished to work with her, who wished to receive the teaching which it was her task to transmit, alive and breathing, into the life of this world, this earth—this individual human being in front of her, who was sometimes me.

I soon learned, but had not yet experienced, that she was bringing what Gurdjieff had said was his "whim," although actually among his deepest aims: *to bring to mankind a new conception of God.*[60]

This Other Attention

Again and again, a hundred times, a thousand times, it seemed, she spoke about an energy that comes from above, from a higher part of the mind, that needs to pass into the body. The body, she said, was built for that, made for that. What we were searching for, the transformation from puppet into man, was meant to take place in the body, not simply in the mind or the emotions. And this about the body had been forgotten in the world, everywhere it had been forgotten. The body was built to serve that energy, to be incarnated by that energy.

But it was not easy. It was very difficult. And there were no techniques, no fixed methods. At the same time it had to be accomplished on this earth, in this human body. Help poured out from her into one's own heart and mind and into the first generation of Gurdjieff's pupils who now had turned to her and in whom I began to sense something uniquely real and living, rich in living weight and a kind of conscious organic materiality, something behind the still existing personalities of all of them. I had never imagined that something so real in human beings could be so obvious and so invisible at the same time. When I had seen these pupils for the first time years ago, all I saw were more or less interesting men and women with many of the ordinary traits of all ordinary people. But now when I looked at them, I often perceived something quite different behind their sharply defined personalities. It was a secret perception of a secret something within the body and soul of a human being— what was it? I didn't know. I couldn't name it. I saw them react and talk and argue and sometimes hurry about like anyone else. But I was seeing something else in them as well. And I was seeing it by means of a new instrument of perception in myself which now awakened in me from time to time, sometimes without my even recognizing it.

When this higher energy, this higher attention coming from above or from a higher part of the mind, was being spoken about, I tried to follow what was being said. I tried to experience it. But what did that mean? Mostly, I was honest enough to see that I was not experiencing it. But the idea itself brought such hope, such interest—as though the key to the whole of human life had been found. There was an intimation of great hope when it was acknowledged that it was difficult and that it was necessary to see and actively accept the truth that one could not reach it, touch it, be touched by it. And even if for a moment perhaps it did touch us, it was gone in an instant. Something in us was not developed enough to allow it to stay. That something that was not developed enough was, among other things, our *ordinary* attention! What I called attention was a world away from that other level of attention, which she spoke of, in seemingly paradoxical language, as conscious attention. What? Wasn't attention by definition conscious?

Again and again, I realized these two simultaneous truths—the greatness of the idea of this higher attention that was meant to permeate the human body, and at the same time the inescapable fact—which I only later was helped to name—that my own attention was a world away from it. My own attention was something I could work with, I could intend something with it, I could put it on this or that. But this other attention was only something I could allow to enter, something which I needed to receive. This tense body composed of egoistic contractions and uncontrolled thoughts and anxious desires could not receive it, except perhaps for an instant, and then it is gone.

Gone, but leaving behind, perhaps, like the wake of a great ship, a wave of deep yearning, a yearning that could only arise when one had been actually touched by this . . . this what? What to call it?

A yearning that itself was fragile and vanished all too quickly in the rough and tumble of everyday life—even in the very moment one walked or spoke or even moved one's head or opened one's eyes.

All this time the wall remained that separated the professor from the seeker. It was only later that I was able to make comparisons with other teachings with awareness of the danger of doing so. It was later that I realized that what I had studied about practices of meditation or inner discipline seemed to make no mention of the immense difficulty of this kind of work. Difficulty? Impossibility was more like it. And as for the new religions that had entered the margins of our culture, starting in San Francisco, the whole tenor of their message was that whatever they were speaking about, it was actually easy—in any case, quite possible.

I was of course aware that in the heart of the great contemplative, esoteric traditions—writings from which were more and more appearing in print—the immense difficulty of such inner work in prayer or meditation was spoken of again and again. In the writings by and about the early Christians in the desert of North Africa there was constant mention of one's absence from God and the need to feel most deeply the sorrow of that absence. The need for tears, divine sorrow watering the impulse of bottomless prayer, was in the cries of the Psalmist in the Old Testament—Why do you hide your face, O Lord? It was in Christ's last words, "Why hast Thou forsaken me?" It was in the Sufi begging in his simple white garment, waiting, waiting for

God. It was in the doubts of Arjuna on the battlefield of life in the Bhagavad Gita; it was in the tales, if not in the doctrine, of the Zen Buddhists sweeping floors for forty years or standing outside in the snow waiting to be allowed in by the Master—to the point, so the legend once went, of cutting off one's own arm as a gesture of need and yearning.

Yes, it was all there in the traditions. But the professor who deeply felt this aspect of the traditions, who even wept with those who wept in the texts—the professor was mercifully kept on one side of the wall, held apart from mixing what he was reading with the realities of his own inner work of seeing and re-membering. As for California's "new religions," many of them, the professor knew that the apparent doctrine of easiness was somehow superficial. Yet even some of the authentic teachers within these new religions were quoted as saying one had "only" to recognize the Brahman, the Godhead, the Buddha nature within oneself in order to be delivered from the torments of the ego. The wall protected me from that as well—thanks to the compassionate rigor of John Pentland. I was able to hear about this higher consciousness or Selfhood without allowing this great half-truth of easy awakening to influence my attitude toward the intense struggle that was demanded in my own inner work.

And again, yes, the professor, filled with respect and love for the theological and mystical traditions of the world, now knew a great deal about the traditional "attributes" of God. They were no longer just hollow philosophical words. The professor knew a great deal about the names of God, that is, the aspects of God's perfection: love, compassion, mercy, wisdom, justice. The Lord our healer, the Lord our master, the Lord Commander, the Bridegroom, the Bright Morning Star of the Old Testament. The Deliverer, the Door, the God Who Sees Me, the Teacher, the True Light—and countless other names, qualities, from the Judeo-Christian tradition. And the ninety-nine names of God in Islam: the Compassionate, the Merciful, the King, the Source of Peace, the Provider, the Forgiving, the Avenger, the Guide. . . . And the gods of Hinduism, all aspects of the One God: the intimate Bhagavan, the impersonal absolute, Ishvara; the invisible trinity of Brahma the creator, Siva the destroyer, Vishnu the maintainer . . . and the countless incarnations of the Buddha throughout endless time, always bringing to man the work of inner freedom . . .

The professor, the writer, the flesh-and-blood human being living in this world appreciating the truths of the great religions, nevertheless had mercifully been helped to maintain a wall of separation protecting my own inner search without mixing it with religion, which, in my secret cave, I did not believe in. In my inner cave I was still a modern man and a child of our era. The teaching I was following allowed me to be free of religion, free of "God." And thereby to work toward something sacred in my own self and in my life.

I see now that had I not kept to that separation, had I not been constantly helped to see my own self-deceptions and egoism, I could easily have translated the idea of the higher energy of Attention into a sort of new mysticism, a belief system in which one might hear about God without even knowing that one had not really experienced God: living and dying without realizing that a deep feeling for higher truths and great ideas could even be an illusion that masked the lack of actual experience. The world—or in any case, I myself—did not need yet one more "mystical" tradition.

Again and again when I heard Madame de Salzmann speak about this higher attention, I felt invited to try to experience it as she spoke. And again and again the way she spoke showed me that I was not *able* to experience it. Even as she spoke of it as the one force, the one energy that could bring all my parts together, the one energy that gave meaning to human life, the energy we were created to receive and manifest as fully human beings— even as she spoke simply and clearly in this way, she showed us that we were not experiencing it. Most mercifully of all, we were guided to see that lack, that absence, not to hide from it, not to pretend, not to become "mystics."

It was a suffering of a kind I had never known before. But, still, the suffering was partly in my mind, in my ego. How could it be that I could not experience this one most essential force? In fact, I did not really know what it was that I was unable to contact. And I didn't know that I didn't know. There were moments when I came in contact with some fine vibration, something strong in my awareness. But again and again I was helped to see that it was not what she was speaking about.

But not only was I not discouraged, I became more and

more serious and interested. Everything I understood to be my full life was being nourished by this teaching. I was able to live with the idea of a higher energy because as an idea it explained so much of the teaching's truly astonishing elements and also because it explained the real predicament of human life on earth.

Once I was sitting in a room with a group of people, listening to her speak. For one fleeting second or microsecond, an indescribable, subtle force gently touched every cell in my body, every hope in my heart, every question in my mind. Or should I say simply, something truly sacred appeared in me and disappeared even as it appeared—like a thousand fine particles of silent light. My heart joyfully rested; my body surrendered all its tension; my mind stopped as wind stops for a second when it changes direction. *I am.*

I don't remember where I was sitting, whether it was in the front row or behind other people. But in that very microsecond she quickly turned her eyes to me and said, simply and undramatically, "That was a good moment."

CHAPTER TWENTY

Conclusion: What the Religions Call God

Where the danger is greatest,
there the helping powers grow.

—HÖLDERLIN

From that time forward there were more "good moments," at first only in her presence, under her guidance, and in later years searching on my own or in the company of others like myself. Almost always such experiences were fleeting, vanishing in the very instant that they appeared. Bringing with them a fusion of joy and sorrow—joy in what had been given, sorrow in that one could not hold it or serve it.

It was not long after the first such experience that I heard her use the word "God" in reference to the energy she was speaking about. Her exact words were "what the religions call God." As I have said, with these words something electric flashed through the wall separating my two lives. What had been an opaque border between the philosopher rich in ideas and the seeker poor in faith and understanding now began to be transformed into a kind of membrane between two existences within a growing life that contained them both. The philosophical and religious idea of God in all its complexity and history was now "occupied," inhabited by an intense new quality of personal experience, like an embryo suddenly receiving a soul and waiting to be born.

And I began to recognize that the idea of God was everywhere in the teaching of Gurdjieff, including the whole of his great written work, *Beelzebub's Tales to His Grandson.*[61] I had already worked my way through that "flying cathedral"[62] of a book several times and had of course seen these many references to God under many designations. But the book's form and voice is such that I never connected what Gurdjieff called by that name with what the religions and philosophies of the world meant by it. And so Gurdjieff's idea of God was never captured by my philosopher's revolving thought and imaginings, never reduced to a mere idea among ideas, an insight among insights, a uniquely "interesting" piece of furniture in the crystal palace of the Emperor of Concepts. Now, however, the content of the philosopher's mind was being bathed in the calm light of the real, hitherto unknown, experiences that had been granted to me.

But the current flows the other way as well. These experiences, fleeting though they were, yet containing more authority than anything else in my life, were themselves illuminated by what God has meant in the spiritual life of humanity. An immense respect and wonder appears in front of the discoveries and teachings of the religions of the world. What inconceivable level and extent of inner experience must have been granted to the great masters whose being and whose teachings over the millennia created the world's religions in every corner and epoch of the life of man?

What do these great lives show us of what is possible for man when he awakens? "Man's possibilities are very great," said Gurdjieff. "You cannot conceive even a shadow of what man is capable of attaining. But nothing can be attained in sleep."[63]

We know of only a few of these greatly awakened men and women who shook the whole world. And, within the confines of each religious tradition, we know of relatively few of the countless spiritual geniuses who transformed the inner and outer life around them. Some have become mythic figures, while for others we have the external lineaments of flesh-and-blood biographies. We have the legendary or mythic figures of Moses, Christ, Mohammed. We have the countless, nameless flesh-and-blood rishis of India as well as such individuals as Ramakrishna and Ramana Maharshi in our present era. There is the endless line and endless number of lines of guides and teachers stretching from the beginning of history to the present, including the great lineages of Buddhist sages and saints, many acting in the world here and now around us. And from within our own Western culture there exist the prophets and rabbinic masters in the long history of Judaism, and the saints and mystics of two thousand years of Christianity. And much, much else, always and everywhere in the life of this planet, our earth. What was the nature of their experience? Could what they have said about God be in great measure based on how that energy acted within themselves? To what extent did they come to understand God through the inconceivable but fully human experience of a higher conscious energy acting, incarnating within themselves? We may even go so far as asking: *To what extent is humanity's entire concept of how God is supposed to act in the world of man a greatly imagined projection of how the higher Attention acts within the human body?*

And, if that is so, how could the human race have ever dreamt that God could act in a merciful, just manner in the human world without the presence of individual men and women who have received the inward God of consciousness within their own human frame? That is the real unrecognized illusion about religion in our world—not the illusion of God's existence that Freud attempted to expose. The deeper, widespread illusion is that God can and should act mercifully and justly in human history without the "instrument" of God-inhabited human beings.

Then we are on the verge of saying, knowing, the shocking truth that God needs not just man, but *awakened man,* in order to act as God in the human world. Without this conscious energy on the earth it may not be possible for divine justice, mercy, or compassion to enter the lives of human beings. Are war, violence, chaos, fantasy, dreams, wasted years, meaningless-ness, cruelty and barbarism what they are in our world because so few human beings exist who in themselves incarnate the action within their own human frame of the great conscious forces and laws of creation and conscious evolution?

And by this we are not speaking only of actions conventionally acknowledged as spiritual, or charitable, or self-sacrificing. We are speaking of sometimes invisible manifestations of powerful, impartial intelligence or organizational justice and steely competence, of invisible, non-egoistic love and help offered at crucial, sometimes subtle, "crossroads" of another individual's life, or the life even of a nation. We are speaking even of something unknown, the unknown influence of fully human *presence* in a situation or in the world. In short, we are speaking of the force of consciousness—of, shall we say, the many names of Attention.

We must not be afraid to follow this idea further—based as it is not on speculation or blind belief or dogma or mystical reports or childhood projections or unanchored metaphysical extravagances or sterile analytical deductions or philosophical arguments, however subtle and intricate.

That is no longer enough and never has been. We are not speaking of blind faith. We are not speaking of the poetic persuasion even of a Rumi or a Kierkegaard; we are not speaking of Plato or Kant or the myths and spiritual teaching stories that we may have heard with such joyous incomprehension.

No. We are speaking of and from experience, inner empiricism. For how in fact does that greater energy act within a man or woman? What are its attributes inwardly, within the human being? Intrapsychically, intra-organically?

Is God a God of love? But when the whole of oneself is touched by that great inner Attention, then love can touch all of one's inner world and enable a human being to bring forth toward another the sustained manifestation of non-egoistic love.

Is God a God of compassion? But when I am compassionate toward all my own parts, my own weaknesses, my own inner lives yearning to obey a higher Unity, my feelings and actions and perceptions can serve the impulse of compassion toward man or animal or any of the sentient life of our world. Such compassion is the attribute not of my ordinary mind or heart or body; these parts operating outside the energy of Attention often end their actions in conflict or distraction or hesitation or hypocrisy, engulfed as these actions are by the egoism that pretends to be the master—the usurper-king of a thousand ancient legends.

Is there only the One God—of Judaism, of Christianity, of Islam? The one state of Awakening of Buddhism? The One Absolute Brahman above and within all the countless gods of Hinduism? Always and everywhere the religions of man speak of the highest reality which it is man's duty to obey. And always and everywhere they warn us not to take the creature for the Creator, not to give our hearts and minds to anything less than the One God, the State of Awakening, the Absolute Mind of the universe. Again and again the language of the religions commands, invites us to worship only God, not gods; to seek the one force that everything within our being yearns to obey and to serve. Are our religions not speaking also of an *inward monotheism?* Not to regard as our "Lord" our better (but lesser) states of understanding or faith, and certainly not our concepts or dreams of God, which may well be illusions, "idols," however "sacred."

Yet at the same time there are the *methods* of religion, the practices, the rites and rituals, the steps along the way, the stations of the cross, the orders of angels and archangels and seraphim, the gradations of awakening, the intermediate stars under the blazing firmament of the one Sun, the universe of gods and demons, rakshasas and dakinis, teachers and *their* teachers and their teacher's teachers—a great chain of vertical being, one level of awakening and love calling to the level below and calling upward to the level above. This picture, too, of a universe of intermediate beings between God and Man and between Man and Hell is rooted in inward experience—the age-old experience of life as a guided path, a way handed down in ever new language from ancient times to the present moment. There is the idea of a path, an inner work, leading step by step to the ability to receive "what the religions call God." And there is help at every step, from others whose essence-obligation it is to transmit the Way to those who come after them. This aspect of religion has been largely forgotten in the West—it is only now just beginning to emerge again out of the shadows of the symbolic language that has not been received inwardly as the promise and the vision of inner evidence and proof of what we are and are meant to be. But this great idea (some call it "esoteric") of intermediate levels of being in the universe can only become real through the experience within ourselves of the vertical chain of being stretching between God and the earth and even below the earth—in a word, "Jacob's Ladder."

Is God a God of Justice? How can we still think such a thing after the twentieth century? And even yesterday's headlines? Surely in our own lived time we have seen from the undeniable outer experience of plural genocides, to name what is most overpoweringly obvious, that any idea of God acting justly in history is defeated by the world we live in and which, no doubt, we have always lived in. And in our hearts, even in hearts that may be filled by pure faith, surely there is also a "cave of absence" where we confront the fact of man's widespread unbearable cruelty to man—often under the name of God Himself. We confront the fact that man is not what he was created to be. Let us say it clearly: Man is not yet Man. In the words of my beloved Tibetan friend: "How many human beings do you really see?"

But where does injustice—which human beings understandably attribute to God and therewith often reject the existence of God altogether—where does the injustice of God begin?

It begins in man. Man cannot be compelled to be just. Man cannot be compelled to be just in the same way that in the larger world of nature and the infinite universe God Himself is just. The infinite universe exists as an immediate manifestation, creation, expression—the great Word—of that which is highest. In our modern language it can be called an energy. Formless, pure, free energy, freely obeying the laws that It, He, or She created. Nature is just, the universe is just, even as it embraces the incomprehensible fact of chance in the quantum world; the universe is ordered and aligned in the mysteriously perfect intelligibility that is given to the human mind to know and the human soul to incarnate in its freely chosen act of attention.

God, in this sense, may be understood to be, among many other things, pure conscious energy, so conscious that it loves and forgives and judges in one instantaneous, infinite act. Everywhere through the endless space of the universe there exists, shall we say, this Divine Attention which everything obeys without question.

But it was, so the legends say, in the creation of Man that something new arose in the universal order (and Man no doubt exists in many elsewheres and perhaps in many forms throughout the universe)—I say, in Man something new had to appear, something that can and must *choose* to obey. It is in this sense that Man is everywhere—in nature, in the earth, in the planets, the stars and all the cosmic entities. Everything has Man hidden within it.

Wherever the process of cosmic creation is taking place, there is, and must be, a specifically human energy, filling, as it were, the stages and steps in the descent and manifestation of what it is that originally emanates from the Source. It is at these everywhere-appearing junctures in the cosmic and planetary world that Man is created and needed as the microcosmic God, the "image and likeness of God," whose work it is to "make straight the ways of the Lord."

Man must choose; that power and gift is his essence. And the instrument, the principal instrument of his choice is his uniquely human attention. But as he is now, man on earth is a being without Attention. His body, the cells and tissues of his body obey only the attention of the animal or the plant or the mineral within him. Man's being, as he is now, cannot obey his mind; it is his mind that obeys his body, which is of the animal or the plant or the mineral.

The countless names of God in Judaism, Christianity, Islam, the hundred million gods of Hinduism, the infinite number of Buddhas in all the aeons of the universe: among all these names, very many can now be understood as characteristics of the manner in which the higher Attention acts within the developed and developing human body.

Can this understanding help us to renew our understanding of God? For those of us who are not graced by purity of heart and pure faith—such people still exist silently among us—for much of the rest of the modern world, we must understand God in a new way with a new language adapted to our modern minds and education, adapted to our familiarity with abstract scientific language. We can say, then, that for us one of the names of God is Attention, the Attention that fills the world and the universe and that Man is created to incarnate in himself so that he can freely obey and be as God in the created world of his own body and thereby manifest toward man and nature what is needed from him.

"That which is truly human is beyond human strength," says

the spiritual philosopher Emmanuel Levinas.[64] This means that it is of the essence of Man to incarnate the highest energy of the universe.

Understanding God now in this way, understanding Man now in this way, we can receive and interpret the forces of the new atheism which has lately expressed itself so provocatively in our culture. We can accept it with a transformed understanding of its possible function, holding in our hands a quite different mirror to it. When we look into the mirror at the new, widely published atheism, articulated as it may be by scientifically trained minds, some of whom no doubt value truth above all superstition, might we not see and hear the holy echoes of the purgation of illusion and fantasy from our concept of God; the exposure of the superficiality of our so-called beliefs; the masks our minds put over our inability to be what we are meant to be; the masks by which we conceal from ourselves our mental and emotional passivity? In the new atheism which perhaps exists in many of us down in our metaphysical subconsciousness, in our own "cave of absence," there emerges in our culture the old and ancient disillusioned longing for the Higher. And not only that. In the name of truth, as it was with the radical empiricists such as David Hume, we may see the precious human enterprise of tearing down all pretense, all illusions, all religious self-deception as an essential purgation of the human mind and heart.

And it is just in that place of absence, the absence of false belief, in that empty space of bittersweet realism, it is just there that great care must be taken not to allow new illusions to emerge, masquerading as the love of truth, but actually representing the very same qualities of arrogance and self-deception that were originally driven out of the temple.

That bittersweet absence of illusion and self-deception, that empty space swept clean by astringent skepticism and purgatorial self-honesty: here perhaps is a truly sacred space in our otherwise self-deceived, chaotic world. In that sacred space, within the individual and within a civilization, and only in such a space, can the new birth be seeded from some source higher than we know, a source searching for us even more than we are searching for it. I will call it, if I may, God—the God whose place has been made ready, paradoxically, by the honest skepticism about God-in-quotation-marks.

Modern man has often identified what is highest in himself with the powers of reason, of rationality purged of blind faith and superstition—blind faith and superstition that itself is of course a mask covering our fears and violence and childish anxieties.

But our rationality has shown us that it is not the master of our lives and our manifestations. The human heart and body do not obey the rationality that our modern world worships. Science does not bring morality, does not bring love, does not bring justice—except perhaps in the dreams of the honest noble humanists who once turned to science and philosophical rationalism in order to change the world, in order to stop wars, in order to bring justice to the world.

It has not happened and it cannot happen. Scientific reason

is not of itself the highest energy of the human psyche. It represents a power within the mind that itself is, shall we say, "given" to man in order to serve as an instrument of conscience, the voice of God.

Yet this scientific rationalism, rooted in logic, mathematics, sense-perception, common sense, wonder, anger at human stupidity and cruelty—this militant scientific rationalism may be welcomed as a purgative force, freeing us to look once again at our concept not just of God but of Man; and not just of Man but of this man or woman here, now, myself.

And here we come finally to the essential conclusion. In myself are all the horrors of man. In my own manifestations I see the eruption of the forces that, left to themselves, without the powers of "God"—love, compassion, justice, rigor and mercy—without the higher energies of universal creation, will master and destroy human life even as they master and destroy my own individual human life. What, after all, is the meaning of my own human life if I live without the yearning for "what the religions call God"? What is the meaning of our lives if we cannot love, cannot be just, cannot hate only what is evil and cannot love only what is good? What is the meaning of our lives if we live enmeshed in the troubled sleep of fear, resentment, fantasy, cruelty, sentimental stupidity or even bloated, arrogant atheism that succumbs to the essence of the very illusions it has honorably sought to expose—namely, the worship of a false god that has sought to usurp the place of the real God?

We cannot blame religion for the evils of "religion." We

cannot blame God for the injustices and indifference of "God." Nature and the universe will go their way. Despite our wars, our brutality, our despoiling of nature—as well as our personal blindness, suggestibility, intoxication, egoism, failures, bitter successes, cocoons of pleasure/pain—we may be sure that the great laws of Nature roll on, adjusting the Earth to our failure to be Man, and eventually, perhaps, looking elsewhere on other worlds for real and true Man to take his place.

But to return to atheism. Might we allow "atheism" to challenge our passive, hypocritical, or superstitious beliefs in order to make room for ideas and thinking that can nourish the human soul in the way that breathing nourishes the human body? Might we allow honest atheism without seeding into our culture and into the minds of our children toxic concepts of what we are and what reality is? By toxic ideas, I mean ideas that deny the higher nature within ourselves that is still calling to us; concepts that smother the sense of wonder, the sense of the Higher in nature and in ourselves waiting to enter our lives. Such toxic concepts are now everywhere, presuming to be realistic only because they fight against an equally toxic religious arrogance.

The growing human being—child or adult—has need for ideas that nourish the search for Truth and the development of the Will to the Good, that nourish the sense of the sacred in nature and, above all, in ourselves. It may not be necessary for everyone to enter the path of inner work, leading to the opening to the true *I Am* within. But it may very well be necessary for the doors to be open to those who are touched by the great wish that leads to the personal search for God, whether that search takes place in the hidden heart of our own ancient teachings; or in the still living practical mysticism of Eastern teachings; or in the rediscovered path leading to the awakening of Conscious Attention; or in ways still, for all we know, hidden and waiting to be "switched on" in our civilization.

Both in our Earth and in our personal lives—we are perhaps at an unimaginably critical juncture in the life of man on Earth.

We cannot wait for very long. The time remaining is very short, is it not?

Coda

Go out one clear starlit night to some open space and look up at the sky, at those millions of worlds overhead. Remember that perhaps on each of them swarm millions of beings, similar to you or perhaps superior to you in their organization. Look at the Milky Way. The earth cannot even be called a grain of sand in this infinity. It dissolves and vanishes, and with it, you. Where are you? And is what you want simply madness?

Before all these worlds ask yourself what are your aims and hopes, your intentions and means of fulfilling them, the demands that may be made upon you and your preparedness to meet them.

A long and difficult journey is before you, you are preparing for a strange and unknown land . . .

Remember where you are and why you are here.

Do not protect yourselves and remember that no effort is made in vain.

And now you can set out on the way.

—G. I. GURDJIEFF, *Views from the Real World*[65]

Faith cannot be given to man. Faith arises in a man and increases in its action in him not as the result of automatic learning, that is, not from any automatic ascertainment of height, breadth, thickness, form and weight, or from the perception of anything by sight, hearing, touch, smell or taste, but from understanding.

Understanding is the essence obtained from information intentionally learned and from all kinds of experiences personally experienced . . .

Yes, Professor, knowledge and understanding are quite different. Only understanding can lead to being, whereas knowledge is but a passing presence in it. New knowledge replaces the old and the result is, as it were, a pouring from the empty into the void.

One must strive to understand; this alone can lead to our Lord God.

—G. I. GURDJIEFF, *Meetings with Remarkable Men*[66]

Notes

1. Sigmund Freud, *The Future of an Illusion.*

2. Søren Kierkegaard, *Kierkegaard's Concluding Unscientific Postscript,* trans. David F. Swenson and Walter Lowrie (Princeton, N. J.: Princeton University Press, 1944), p. 221.

3. Ibid., pp. 221–22.

4. Daisetz T. Suzuki, *Zen and Japanese Culture* (Princeton, N. J.: Princeton University Press, 1970), pp. 107–108.

5. Kierkegaard, p. 217.

6. *The Confessions of St. Augustine,* trans. Edward B. Pusey (New York: Pocket Books, 1952), p. 1.

7. Gershom G. Scholem, *Major Trends in Jewish Mysticism* (New York: Schocken Books, 1961), p. 17.

8. Ibid., p. 25.

9. Ibid., p. 139.

10. A brilliant translation of this towering text has been brought forth by Daniel C. Matt in four volumes: *The Zohar,* trans. Daniel C. Matt (Stanford, Calif.: Stanford University Press, 4 volumes dating from 2004 to the present).

11. Moses Maimonides, *The Guide for the Perplexed,* trans. M. Friedländer (New York: Dover Publications, 1956).

12. Martin Buber, *I and Thou,* trans. Ronald Gregor Smith (New York: Charles Scribner's Sons, 1958).

13. Martin Buber, *Tales of the Hasidim: Book One and Book Two* (New York: Schocken Books, 1991).

14. Ibid., Book One, p. 251.

15. Ibid., Book One, p. 68.

16. Ibid., Book One, p. 69.

17. Ibid., Book One, p. 77.

18. Ibid., Book Two, p. 253.

19. Rudolph Bultmann, *Primitive Christianity in Its Contemporary Setting* (New York: Meridian Books, 1956).

20. *The Early Christian Fathers,* ed. and trans. Henry Bettenson (London: Oxford University Press,1963).

21. Hans Jonas, *The Gnostic Religion* (Boston: Beacon Press, 1958), p. 58.

22. Bultmann, p. 71.

23. Ibid., pp. 71–72.

24. Ibid., p. 73.

25. Romans 7:6–25; 8:2.

26. Karl Barth, *The Epistle to the Romans* (London: Oxford University Press, 1972), p. 268.

27. Ibid., p. 268.

28. Ibid., p. 269.

29. Ibid., p. 269.

30. Jonas, p. 58.

31. Ibid., p. 66.

32. Ibid., p. 70.

33. Ibid., p. 70.

34. Ibid., p. 89.

35. Thomas de Hartmann, *Our Life with Mr. Gurdjieff* (New York: Cooper Square Publishers, 1964); several augmented and revised editions have been published since. The final, definitive edition: Thomas and Olga de Hartmann, *Our Life with Mr. Gurdjieff* (Sandpoint, Idaho: Sandpoint Press, 2008).

36. P. D. Ouspensky, *In Search of the Miraculous* (New York: Harcourt, 2001).

37. Ibid., Chapter 1.

38. Ibid., pp. 122–140.

39. As opposed, that is, to the utilitarian "as if" frameworks of Newtonian and non-Newtonian theoretical calculation.

40. Lobsang Phuntsok Lhalungpa, "Buddhism in Tibet," in *The Path of the Buddha*, ed. Kenneth W. Morgan (New York: Ronald Press, 1956), pp. 237–306.

41. These talks are collected in Jacob Needleman and Dennis Lewis, eds., *Sacred Tradition and Present Need* (New York: The Viking Press, 1975).

42. *The Life of Milarepa*, trans. Lobsang Lhalungpa (London: Arkana Books, 1992).

43. Michel de Salzmann, "Seeing: the Endless Source of Inner Freedom," in *Material for Thought* (San Francisco: Far West Editions), vol. 14, p. 14.

44. Immanuel Kant, *Immanuel Kant's Critique of Pure Reason*, trans. Norman Kemp Smith (London: Macmillan and Co., Ltd., 1953), p. 7.

45. D. T. Suzuki, *Zen Buddhism: Selected Writings of D. T. Suzuki*, ed. William Barrett (New York: Doubleday, 1956), p.8.

46. *Treatise*, Part IV, Section VI. This famous passage entitles Hume to be designated as the first specifically modern practitioner of inner empiricism. When he honestly looked into his own mind and could find no self there, he was stepping onto the shore of a vast country of self-observation—a country, a world of which the modern mind has remained almost entirely ignorant, contenting itself with remaining on the dry, barren edges of that inner world, complacently building sandcastles of relativistic philosophy and naively scientific psychology. Yet who could have known that Hume's greatest discovery was the significance of the practice of self-observation, which could have brought him the only possible answer to his electrifying skepticism? He would no doubt have discovered that many of the great questions mankind has asked of the outer world can be answered only farther "inland" in the inner world. In any case, the similarity here to the

Buddhist teaching about the illusion of selfhood is unmistakable and, in fact, there is some striking, speculative evidence that the young Hume was acquainted with the Buddhist view and may even have been influenced by it. This evidence is plausibly offered in a recent article by Alison Gopnik, presented at the Meeting of the World History Association, London, June 2008, and the American Philosophical Association Pacific Division, April 2009. The article is entitled: "Could David Hume have known about Buddhism? Charles Francis Dolu, the Royal College of La Flèche, and the global Jesuit intellectual network."

47. *Enquiry*, conclusion.

48. Richard J. Bernstein, *Philosophical Profiles* (Philadelphia: University of Pennsylvania Press, 1986), p. 265.

49. With his characteristic scientific honesty and precision, Freud was careful to speak of religion as an "illusion," not as a "delusion." To speak of a belief as a delusion was to dogmatically affirm it to be false. But to call religion an illusion was only to say (and this of course was already a great deal) that it was very probably false, but that it could conceivably be true. The mirage of water in the desert was the example of an illusion. It could conceivably be true that the thirsty traveler was seeing an oasis, but all things considered, it was highly improbable. Freud's revolutionary work *The Future of an Illusion* powerfully characterized religious belief in God as comparable to a mirage engendered by prescientific humanity's helplessness and desperate craving for a feeling of security vis-à-vis the overwhelming forces of nature.

50. René Guénon, *The Crisis of the Modern World* (Ghent, NY: Sophia Perennis, 1996).

51. P. D. Ouspensky, *A New Model of the Universe* (New York: Dover Publications, 1997).

52. 2 Peter 1:20.

53. Isaiah 28:9–10.

54. William James, *The Varieties of Religious Experience* (New York: Penguin Books, 1985), pp. 27–28.

55. Ibid., p. 46.

56. Anonymous, *The Cloud of Unknowing* (New York: Doubleday, 1973).

57. This oft-quoted saying is, as far as I have seen, inevitably attributed to Saint Augustine, but no one seems to know where in his writings it is actually to be found, and at least one eminent Augustine scholar seriously questions the attribution.

58. G. I. Gurdjieff, *Meetings with Remarkable Men* (New York: Penguin Books, 1985).

59. René Daumal, *Mount Analogue* (New York: Penguin Books, 1959), one of the most vibrant and creative portrayals of Gurdjieff's teaching.

60. Gurdjieff is quoted as having said this in Philip Mairet, *A. R. Orage* (New York: University Books, 1966), p. 105.

61. G. I. Gurdjieff, *Beelzebub's Tales to His Grandson* (New York: Penguin Books, 1992 and 2006).

62. A phrase coined by Pamela Travers. See her *George Ivanovitch Gurdjieff* (Toronto: Traditional Studies Press, 1973).

63. *In Search of the Miraculous*, p. 145.

64. Emmanuel Levinas, *Nine Talmudic Readings* (Bloomington: Indiana University Press, 1994), p. 100.

65. G. I. Gurdjieff, *Views from the Real World* (New York: Penguin Books, 1984), pp. 58–59.

66. G. I. Gurdjieff, *Meetings with Remarkable Men* (New York: Jeremy P. Tarcher, 1985), pp. 240–42.

Index

About the Author

The author of *Why Can't We Be Good?*, *The American Soul*, *Money and the Meaning of Life*, *The Heart of Philosophy*, *The New Religions*, and *Lost Christianity*, among other books, Jacob Needleman is professor of philosophy at San Francisco State University and former director of the Center for the Study of New Religions at the Graduate Theological Union, Berkeley, California. He was educated at Harvard, Yale, and the University of Freiburg, Germany. He has also served as research associate at the Rockefeller Institute for Medical Research and was a research fellow at Union Theological Seminary. In addition to teaching and writing, he serves as a consultant in the fields of psychology, education, medical ethics, philanthropy, and business. He has also been featured on Bill Moyers's PBS television series *A World of Ideas*. He lives with his wife, Gail, in Oakland, California.